RIVERS ALWAYS REACH THE SEA

ALSO BY MONTE BURKE

Lords of the Fly

Saban

4th and Goal

Sowbelly

Leaper (coeditor)

Atlantic Salmon Treasury, 75th Anniversary Edition (coeditor)

RIVERS ALWAYS REACH THE SEA

ANGLING STORIES

MONTE BURKE

PEGASUS BOOKS
NEW YORK LONDON

RIVERS ALWAYS REACH THE SEA

Pegasus Books, Ltd.
148 W 37th Street, 13th Floor
New York, NY 10018

Copyright © 2025 by Monte Burke

These stories originally appeared in the following publications:
*Garden & Gun, The Drake, Forbes, ForbesLife, Field & Stream, The FlyFish Journal,
Fly Rod & Reel,* the *Tom Beckbe Field Journal,* and *Gray's Sporting Journal.*

First Pegasus Books edition June 2025

Interior design by Maria Fernandez

All rights reserved. No part of this book may be reproduced in whole or in part
without written permission from the publisher, except by reviewers who may quote
brief excerpts in connection with a review in a newspaper, magazine, or electronic
publication; nor may any part of this book be reproduced, stored in a retrieval system,
or transmitted in any form or by any means electronic, mechanical, photocopying,
recording, or other, or used to train generative artificial intelligence (AI)
technologies, without written permission from the publisher.

Library of Congress Cataloging-in-Publication Data is available.

ISBN: 978-1-63936-899-0

10 9 8 7 6 5 4 3 2 1

Printed in the United States of America
Distributed by Simon & Schuster
www.pegasusbooks.com

For my father,

and

for Justin and Chris

Do not tell fish stories where the people know you; but particularly, don't tell them where they know the fish.

—Mark Twain

There comes a time when you realize that everything is a dream, and only those things preserved in writing have any possibility of being real.

—James Salter

Contents

	Foreword by David DiBenedetto	xi
	Introduction	xiii
1	Fall Run	1
2	The Happiest Man in the World	5
3	Shark Bait	13
4	The Legend of Lefty	17
5	Jamaica Bay	31
6	My Spot, Burned	35
7	First Tarpon	39
8	The Dream-Maker	43
9	Bone Home Me	51
10	X Marks the Spot	55
11	Difficulty	61
12	The Passion of Andy Mill	65
13	Salmon Season	77
14	A Lifetime of Atlantic Salmon in a Day	81
15	Blind Casting	85

16	Power Play	87
17	End of the Season	93
18	The Lion in Winter	99
19	Green Drakes	111
20	Sulphurs	113
21	Thought Rods	117
22	December	123
23	Second-Chance Trout	127
24	Fishing Through a Pandemic	137
25	Tier's Poker	141
26	Brookies Under Broadway	145
27	The Beast	149
28	Toots	161
29	Retrieved	167
30	The Sportsman	177
31	The Last American Howler	183
	Acknowledgments	191

Foreword

There are only a few people in the world that I'd share my secret fishing spots with and one of them is Monte Burke. When he traveled to a beach resort in the Lowcountry of South Carolina that I know well, I told him about a nearby marsh flat that holds not only tailing redfish on big flood tides but also sheepshead. I call it Land of the Giants. I won't even share its location with some members of my family. But Monte gets it. He understands the unwritten rules of serious fishermen, which among other things involves a Mafia-like code of silence and a deep respect for the resource. It does not involve selfie sticks.

That's one reason why I've never hesitated to send him on any fishing assignment in the fifteen years I've worked with him, whether he was profiling a legendary tarpon guide or exploring the spring creeks of Chile. When he's working on a story, Monte is as focused on delivering the reporting goods as he is when landing a tarpon on the fly (which he's done numerous times). But that's only half the battle. He takes those notes, both physical and mental, and turns them into some of the best writing on fishing that you can find in print or pixels today. This gem of a book is a collection of that great work spanning twenty-five years.

For the record, ours is a reciprocal relationship. Recently, before I headed to a remote island in the Bahamas that Monte had visited (and fished) quite often, he sent me a detailed report of the local bonefish flats accessible by foot. Under a heading that read "Graveyard Flat," he noted that the fishing was best on in incoming tide early in the morning, before the boat traffic. I showed up as directed, welcomed by a fleet of waving silver tails. Monte had delivered again.

David DiBenedetto
Editor-in-Chief
Garden & Gun
Charleston, South Carolina

Introduction

I stumbled into this game, this writing thing. For years after college, I didn't have the courage to even try it. I believed, instead, that I should do the responsible thing. So I applied to business schools. Somehow, I even got into one.

But it was in the composing of the essays for those applications that I found something. I was in my early twenties, that period of life when you are just scratching the surface of some sort of real knowledge. And for the first time, really, I was forced to sit down and think deeply about where I'd been, where I was, and where I wanted to go. What I figured out through the process of writing those essays was that I, in fact, did *not* want to go to business school (a visit to the school I got into, which provoked a pit in my stomach, confirmed that notion). What those essays did, instead, was make me realize I desperately wanted to write.

So I decided to do so. I had no idea where to start (a novel sounded like a bit much at the time . . . and still does). But then I remembered the old saw: "write what you know." It's a cliché for a reason.

Like I said, I didn't know much about anything at the time. But I did know I loved to fly-fish. Love is probably not strong enough of a word. I was, and remain, incurably drawn to water. The fly rod has been my dowsing stick.

I deferred a year from that business school. I decided to try to write about a creek, a ribbon of water that most people just drove by without even really noticing it was even there. But it had trout in it. And it had an interesting history, at least in the annals of fly-fishing. I threw everything I had into the piece. It ended up at four thousand words. A tome. I sent it around to all the big magazines. None bit. But a small one finally did, and bought it for $200. That was that. I informed the business school that I wasn't coming (my future father-in-law was, shall we say, not exactly ecstatic about my decision-making skills when it came to potential future income). And I wrote.

For the majority of my "career" (it still feels funny to call it that), writing about fly-fishing has been a side gig, something I did in the margins merely because I loved doing it. I spent almost fifteen years at *Forbes* magazine, doing profiles of entrepreneurs, sports team owners, hedge-fund managers, and CEOs. I wrote books about college football, and continue to do so. But fishing writing was always there. Like Michael Corleone, I could never fully extricate myself from the grasp of some powerful force in my life.

I think what drew me to it was that it is a sport that lends itself to being written about. Because of its biomechanical repetition and the mostly beautiful places in which it is practiced, fly-fishing occasionally puts you in an instinctual, stoned-like trance, that staring-into-a-fire thing that can sometimes encourage a deeper contemplation. It requires patience and the putting together of dozens of little details that make a greater whole, like the words and sentences that comprise a story or a book. It has long lulls filled by internal dialogue, punctuated by sudden moments of high drama that swiftly empty your mind. It has victories, but it's the losses that become seared into memory. Your fly line, when cast properly, even forms an arc.

The sport has kept me sane. I don't mean to suggest I would be in the loony bin without it, but it has provided, over the years, just enough of a respite, a diversion, to keep me keeping on in my "real" life. It has taken me all over the world, to places I would have never gone otherwise—it is one of the world's great passports, a way of experiencing the natural beauty of different countries and continents, not just their urban hearts. Though travel is very fun and something that would be hard to go without, I love my homewaters, too, with ferocity. There is maybe nothing better in the sport than profoundly getting to know a few pieces of water.

INTRODUCTION

I fish differently now. We all do as we age. I am more patient, which has helped me as an angler (and as a father). My angling has not been improved, however, but my tendency to sometimes overthink things a bit and not just trust instinct and bull ahead with utter confidence (this is the reason middle-aged golfers lose their putting prowess). I no longer feel that atavistic urge to catch every fish in the river, as I did when I was younger. But I do still want to catch fish. A taken fly is an essential part of the process, providing the necessary shape and coherence to the journey. And every time a fish takes our fly, it evokes the very first time we felt that electric connection, that one moment that for any serious fly angler has animated everything since.

I come to fly-fishing to stare into that matrix of mangroves, sea, and sky, utterly lost but, somehow, also found. I come to witness the day fade into dusk, when the air is filled with that warm, soft light of Vermeer, and stay on the river until I can no longer see the fish, and only then reluctantly trudge out, water dripping from my waders, under that shotgun blast of stars in the night sky. I come to make sure I'm standing ready when Melville's "great floodgates of the wonder-world" swing wide open.

I come to the rivers and creeks and flats and rips and lakes and ponds of this world now as a petitioner. Heaven's wasted on the dead, as Isbell sang, but fly-fishing is my way of making an attempt to reach for the hem of that garment.

Fly-fishing is, after all, a love story. And like all loves, it needs constant care and maintenance.

The legendary guide Steve Huff once told me that his fishing outfit back in the glory years of the 1970s and '80s in the Florida Keys was "a pair of cutoff jeans and a gold chain."

Things change. Most everyone these days, including Huff himself, is covered head-to-toe with sun protection when fishing. We've evolved, becoming more sensible with our bodies.

And yet, I would argue that we, as a fly-fishing body politic, have become less sensible with the resource and our responsibility to it. We are loving it to death. We view it as just another thing to be used, consumed, exploited. To be sure, I am a part of the problem.

I've had a couple of prominent guides tell me in recent years that they believe it's all over already, that we've passed the point of no return in our fisheries. This is a rather heady and shocking thought, and they may be right, but even if they are, we must stay after it, just in case they're not. I realize it can all make one feel helpless and overwhelmed. It's hard to figure out what one can do, individually, about a warming climate—that hot air for the cool breeze—which is negatively impacting fish, from Atlantic salmon in the north to tarpon in the south. It remains utterly frustrating to realize we seem powerless to solve some of the big, intractable issues, like the wanton, decades-long destruction of the Everglades that's due mainly to just a handful of corporate owners who have bought politicians on both sides of the aisle.

But in the end, we have to try to do *something*. We have to maintain a healthy pessimism of the intellect, but an even healthier optimism of the will. These wild animals and wild places represent our ethical values, and those values, more so than our monetary ones, are essential to our very being.

We have responsibilities now as sportsmen and women, conscious choices to make. We can still play like children on the water, but we must act like grown-ups off it, to paraphrase Marshall Cutchin. Individually, that might mean writing a check to, or doing volunteer work for, a conservation organization that's making a difference. Collectively, it might mean, say, working to kick out those politicians who take money from those destroying the Everglades.

There's more: we don't have to post a picture on social media of every fish we catch (really). We don't have to hook every small bonefish in the school or every tiny rising trout in the pool just to pad our numbers for the bullshitting back at the lodge. We don't have to fish when the water in the river is too warm. Take a deep breath. Turn off the phone. Take the music speaker out of the boat. Take a look around. Listen to the river or the flat. It's telling us something.

1

Fall Run

The rocks on this jetty were once uniform and composed. They say that, long ago, you could drive a car on them, all the way out to the tower at the end, where the greasy cormorants preen their feathers. This is no longer possible. The Long Island Express hit it with hundred-mile-an-hour winds and fifteen-foot swells just a few years after it was built. Then came Hazel, Donna, Esther, Agnes, Gloria, Isabel, Irene, and Sandy, all the nasty girls. The rocks are now jumbled, misshapen. Some have fallen into the water, unattached to the jetty at all. Others wobble in the waves like loose teeth. Such is the fate of all ocean jetties.

It is now navigable only by foot, with care and Korkers. It is one of the great fishing jetties in the Northeast. Maybe I say this because it is the one closest to my apartment.

My fly buddies, Dave and Nick, hit it. This jetty is Dave's baby. He's been coming out for decades, and has caught all sorts of fish from it: stripers, blues, bonito, albies, fluke, skate, weakfish, blackfish, dogfish, even a thirty-pound black drum. Nick is just a northeast saltwater fiend. I once asked him a question about trout fishing and he answered, quite plausibly, "What is that?"

Spin guys love the jetty, too. It is one of the few places in the Northeast where spin and fly fishermen coexist peaceably. There is the tall, dour

German who casts only when necessary and speaks only when spoken to; the Russians with their shaved heads and cauliflower ears; and the young tugboat captain who works two-weeks-on, two-weeks-off so he can fish a lot. He occasionally has to leave the jetty early to take his mother to an Islanders game.

I was out at the tip, all by myself. Not everyone makes the walk all the way out, and I don't blame them. The rocks are dangerous. Every few years, someone dies out here. If you happened to fall in on a strong outgoing tide, there's little chance you'd make it back. At the tip, you feel like you are standing in the middle of the ocean. Before you, the horizon leads to Portugal.

I'd been searching for false albacore for two weeks now. I wanted to catch one without the aid of a boat. It had been three seasons since I'd done that. Getting one from the shore makes you feel like you've earned both the fish *and* the good luck. In my pursuit, I'd made the two-hour drive to the inlet near the East End that's famous for its albie blitzes, enduring dark highways, bad coffee, mediocre sports talk radio, and hours of staring into the water at untroubled bait. In three trips, I'd seen a total of one quick blitz. I was walking at the time, and had committed the cardinal sin of not being prepared: I was reeled up, leaving no line out in my stripping basket, when I saw the fish. They were long gone before I could make a cast.

I'd tried some new spots on the North Shore. One was the former estate of a merchant prince, now owned by the state. The water and beach were beautiful, the bait present. But the blitzes were well out of range. I started to become a bit obsessed. I targeted albies to the exclusion of other species. One morning I saw a spin guy wrestle a big striper from the hissing surf, looking like a man pulling a large suitcase from an airport baggage carousel. But I paid it little mind. Sure, I was physically present at home and work, but my thoughts were on the water. I took much pleasure in the thinking and planning that went into these trips, what Dave and I called "the scheming," which always resumed the very moment I left the water. I enjoyed the scheming so

FALL RUN 3

much that I began to wonder if I "relished the fantasy more than the finished work," as Kesey once wrote.

Nah. I just wanted a shore albie.

That day on the jetty was sunny and mild. One of the joys of fishing the "hardtail" portion of the fall run is the weather. The water is still warm. Wearing shorts is still sometimes the sensible thing to do. The wind was coming from the northwest—Longfellow's Keewaydin. The sea was Caribbean green, as clear and clean looking as I'd ever seen it. I'd heard rumblings on my offline social network of some possible albie sightings in the area. I was thrilled to be alone at the tip, to not have to worry about hooking a spin guy on my backcast.

I looked out over the ocean, smoothed by the wind and the tide, scanning for feeding fish, for birds. Nothing was happening, but I worked out a few casts anyway. It was a good thing I did. My line, perhaps not totally dry from the day before, was kinkier than Rick James. I looped it under my boot and pulled to straighten it out. I left some in my stripping basket, and then sat on a rock and waited.

Soon, though, I began to daydream, something I regrettably don't do much of anymore. I fell into such a trance that nearly an hour went by with no recollection of what I thought or did other than sit and stare. I may have fallen asleep.

I was yanked back into the present by a commotion off the tip. Albies were flinging themselves out of the water, in pursuit of some silversides. Everything became quick. I stood and made a cast, did a series of hand-over-hand strips, and was tight. The fish broke off because I didn't let go of my line in time.

I tied on another fly and scanned the water. Mini-eruptions were happening all around me, but they were well out of range. Birds wheeled about, trying to get a bead on the mayhem created by albies. Everything around seemed locked in on them.

Another pod came in close. I flipped out my fly and hooked one, and was into my backing quickly. As I reeled, I scanned the area for a suitable landing spot. I found a rock close to the water and tailed the fish. I briefly admired its green-blue gleam and the vermicular lines on its back, then let it go. I felt utterly alive. The highs during the fall run come in such small but powerful doses.

I came back again the next day and the day after that and the day after that, in full fever, seeing and catching just enough fish to stoke, but not fully satisfy, the craving. Family members, friends, neighbors, and coworkers all looked at me funny. I wondered if I appeared admirable or pathetic.

Like all my addictions, I took this one too far. I went out on a day when I should have had my ass parked in a chair, working. It was November. I'd heard of reports of albies at Harkers, which usually signaled the end of the run here. At the jetty, the incoming tide was heavy, spuming rough white surf over my favorite fishing rocks. There were no birds and no fish. After twenty minutes of fruitless casting, I sat on a rock and stared at the sea, trying to recapture something I knew was already gone.

2015

2

The Happiest Man
in the World

Dear Thoughtful Reader: A brief word of warning. The word "fuck" is used a lot in this piece. We counted approximately seventy-six instances. If you are easily offended, under the age of eighteen, live in a state with weird sodomy laws, or happen to be sitting down with this on a Sunday before noon, you might want to consider skipping this story. If, however, you appreciate the artful employment of the word by a man who happens to be among its most skillful and profuse users, then by all means read on. Or as Captain Frank would say, "Fucking go for it, man."—Eds

Here's the scene: I'm twenty-five and new to Gotham, a city I swore up and down and all around I would never, ever inhabit. I occupy the smallest room of a gigantic loft apartment near Chinatown shared with three roommates who have seemingly bottomless appetites for takeout and pornography, both of the Asian variety. They all work on Wall Street. I work as an administrative assistant (read: secretary) at an outdoor sports magazine, a job for which I had spurned the yellow brick road of business school. I live with my ten-year-old golden retriever who, somewhat surprisingly, takes to the city well, what with its olfactory riches and legions of overfed, sluggish rats. I am desperately homesick for the life I have left behind, the endless hours, days, months spent tramping the woods and wading the waters of Alabama, North Carolina, Virginia, and Vermont, a type of life that seems impossible to find in this city. Fishing to me becomes something that seems unattainable except by proxy and thus desired with more intensity, much like real Asian women are to my new roommates.

Then one day the phone rings at work. Since I'm the phone-answering wretch, I take the call. The voice on the other end says there's a fishing tournament coming up in Manhattan. The voice is wondering if I want to do a pre-fish, check out the New York Harbor and all its glory, you know, give it a fucking whirl. I immediately think this is a prank call from a college buddy. It's not. It's Captain Frank Crescitelli of Staten Island, New York.

<hr/>

A week later, in the darkness of the early morning, I'm standing at the southernmost tip of the Isle of Manhattan, the site of the original sixteenth-century Native American trading outpost, a place of commerce then and now. I'm with a New York City photographer named Brendan, who has little, if any, fishing experience. We jump on the Staten Island Ferry, a big orange behemoth that smells like a giant urinal mint. The twenty-five-minute ride to the forgotten borough costs twenty-five cents. A few years later, this ferry would ram into the Staten Island docks, killing eleven people and nearly adding another when the pilot tried in vain to die by suicide, slitting his wrists in the cockpit just moments after the accident he caused.

We get to Staten Island in one piece. It's still dark as we walk through the terminal to the parking area. There I lay eyes on Captain Frank for the first time. With his hands in his pockets, he's leaning against his big black Cadillac Escalade with a license plate that reads FINCHASR. He has a waterman's solid build and jet-black hair that cascades down the back of his neck into a perfect mullet. A shit-eating grin is spread across his face, stretching the handlebars of his black mustache.

We hop in. Captain Frank puts the key in the ignition, and we are immediately blasted by Angus Young's opening guitar riff from "Back in Black." Captain Frank doesn't even so much as glance at the volume knob. We communicate like mimes. Brendan and I nod and smile and arch our eyebrows when we give the "thumbs-up" sign. Captain Frank plays air guitar. We are a noise bomb launched through the dark, sleepy streets of Staten Island. I picture our wake rippling through the darkened apartment bedrooms as we pass by, the housewives in hairnets and faded terrycloth robes elbowing their snoring husbands in the ribs, imploring them to *do something 'cause those damn kids are making this neighborhood go to hell.* At one point during the drive Captain Frank grabs hold of my arm and yells over the music: "I FUCKING *LOVE* AC/DC!"

It's five A.M.

We stop at a bagel shop. Inside, the bagel man stands behind the counter and a group of men sit in plastic chairs, wearing plaid flannel shirts and Carhartts and drinking black coffee. For a fleeting moment, I feel like I could be in, say, Wisconsin, surrounded by men—electricians, construction workers—who gather for coffee and bullshitting before putting in an honest eight. Captain Frank greets the group with a "How you doin' fellas?" then picks up some bagels. As we're leaving, one of the coffee drinkers saunters up to the counter and leans on his elbow like a barfly. He looks the bagel man in the eye and says, "I got a joke for you, buddy. So there are these two guys in a canoe, fucking a mongoose . . ." Just then the door shuts, forever depriving me of the punch line.

We shove off from Staten Island's Captain's Marina at six A.M. We fish all day, catching striper after striper, mostly on top with Gurglers. We cast flies beneath "the skirt" (the Statue of Liberty), by the United Nations building in the East River, and off Hoffman and Swinburne Islands, used in the nineteenth century as a quarantine and crematorium, respectively, for sickly immigrants who landed at Ellis Island. At the end of the day, with the boat perched by a stanchion of the Verrazano Bridge, Brendan finally puts down his camera and picks up a spinning rod. He makes a cast. When he reels it in, he spots something stuck on the end of his white jig, something cream-colored, wrinkly, and cylindrical. "Umm, Captain Frank, what's this?" he asks, timidly. Captain Frank quickly yanks the robusto cigar out of his piehole and bellows, "Brendan, fuckin' A, you caught a Coney Island Whitefish!" Which, of course, is a rubber.

It had been many years since Captain Frank had seen one. Its capture brings his story full circle. When Captain Frank was "a little fucker," as he puts it, in the 1960s and '70s, casting from the shores of Staten Island or Brooklyn into waters as defiled as any in the nation, he caught one or two Coney Island Whitefish for every sickly striper. Eden was a mess, the Old Testament fall from grace complete. But Captain Frank held on to his hope that it would turn around, kept faith in the New Testament promise of redemption. He kept fishing. He bought a boat. He shrugged his big shoulders when people openly mocked him for starting a guiding service in the harbor. He founded his own fishing conservation organization. And the stripers came back.

<hr>

A few years ago, Captain Frank and I decided, just for shits and giggles, to do a "hook and cook." We were, of course, fully aware of the health advisories that had been slapped on Hudson River stripers, because of the PCBs (polychlorinated biphenyls, thanks to General Electric plants upstream) the fish host in their fatty tissue. But on principle, we felt it was something we had to do.

I met him early in the morning. We fished very hard. For once our goal was a striper for the table, not for sport. I hadn't fished for food in a long while, and that emphasis brought a whole new awareness, an animistic intensity to the day. We caught many bluefish, and kept a few in the "cocktail" size. We landed a handful of stripers, but no keepers. Near the end of the day, Captain Frank directed the boat to a rip off Swinburne Island, his honeyhole. It was our last chance for a keeper striper. He forsook the fly rod and picked up a spinning rod, tying on an enormous hook. He took a fat, shiny, live menhaden from the baitwell and impaled it through the lips and then cast it out. Then he fell into a Zen-like trance, holding the slack line between his forefinger and thumb, watching the spot in the water where the menhaden swam in wild circles, staring with that middle-distance gaze like one does when driving at night, aware of all things within the halo of headlights and just beyond. I'd never witnessed Captain Frank in this meditative state before. I was used to his jawing and good-natured yelling. He spoke in low conversational tones, coolly giving me instructions on where to point the boat to keep it right on the rip. Live-lining is its own mysterious art. Suddenly he reared back on the rod with force and started to pump and reel. It was a fun fight to watch. After five minutes, it was still a draw. This was a big fish. Eventually Captain Frank got the upper hand, and I helped him net a twenty-pound striper.

We went back to his two-story house on a cul-de-sac in the Tottenville section of Staten Island. I'd never been to any purely residential part of Staten Island before, so I had no idea what to expect. There were kids' bikes lying on their sides in front yards. A Plexiglass backboard and hoop was set up on the street with a few worn basketballs strewn about its base. It reminded me of the suburbs of Chicago.

"Hope you don't mind that I invited a few friends over," Captain Frank said as he filleted the big striper in his garage. Of course I didn't. I went to the guest room to get cleaned up. When I came back downstairs, Captain Frank's "few" friends had shown up. Eight to be exact. The Valentines, the Bittmans, the Sullivans, and the O'Byrnes. They all called him "Frankie," and they all laughed and nodded and stuffed their faces with bluefish cake appetizers as he told off-color jokes between his own huge, messy swigs of Cabernet. His wife Sharon frequently rolled her eyes in a good-natured "that's my Frankie" kind of way. Captain Frank left the party for a few minutes to tuck his two young daughters into bed. The air seemed to have been sucked from the room. Then he reappeared, the party ensued, and we ate the striper, grilled to perfection, PCBs be damned.

After dinner, the men retreated to Captain Frank's basement, which is furnished exactly like a bar. In fact, there is an actual bar, with nearly every type of liquor stocked behind it and a tap that pours Budweiser. There's a pool table and a dartboard.

Captain Frank lit our cigars, and then acted as the bartender. "You're on your own after the first one," he said. Then he turned up the Springsteen so loud that I really couldn't really hear it, I just felt it. "IT'S OK," he yelled. "THE BASEMENT IS SOUNDPROOFED." I was told I played an awful game of pool that night. I was also told that I took a private car home. I recollected neither.

⚊

People genuinely like Captain Frank. They like being around him. He's an optimist and a positive thinker, which are good traits for a fisherman and even better traits for a fishing guide. "Negative people are real fucking downers," he says. He attends Tony Robbins seminars every year with Sharon. It helps him sell insurance (he does part-time work for State Farm). It helps him sell the fishing in New York Harbor. It helps him in general. He's much sought-after as an after-dinner auctioneer, and has done it for years for his annual striper tournament in Manhattan. He's performed for the Yale Fishing Club and for the Montauk Redbone Tournament. His auctioneering style is one of a kind. He starts off in sort of an upbeat conversational tone, speaking directly to the audience, making eye contact, imploring them to open their wallets. There's none of that rapid-fire, barely understandable stuff that the pros do. But when an item isn't receiving the bids he thinks it should, he'll finally break down and say, "C'mon people, somebody fucking buy this thing!"

He's had one failure as an auctioneer. The folks at the Redbone, impressed with his Montauk performance, invited him down to Islamorada in the Florida Keys for the tournament there. On auction night Captain Frank stood up in his wide-lapelled black suit and white shirt and took the mic, barking out the items and their prices to a staid group

THE HAPPIEST MAN IN THE WORLD 11

of men in Nantucket red pants and women in blue hair and natural pearls. The audience just sat there, hands in their laps, in a stunned, "Oh, the *vulgarity!*" silence.

"They didn't fucking get me," says Captain Frank.

In case it's not already apparent, Captain Frank really likes to use the word "fuck." One day on the water I decided to count them. The "fucks," that is. I figured out, based on a sample from a five-minute diatribe concerning an infamous striped bass poacher in the harbor, that Captain Frank uses the word "fuck," or some derivation thereof, once in every five to ten spoken words. He uses it as a noun ("That dude is a fucker"), a verb ("He takes the fish when they're fucking, during the spawn"), and an adjective ("The fucking guy just poaches them all fucking day"). When I suggested he try using it sometime as an "-ly" adverb, he replied: "Fuck that."

Captain Frank and I fished together this past Halloween. Last year on this day, he dressed up in a full Santa Claus suit and fished all day in order to get what turned out to be an awesome grip-and-grin photo for his Christmas card. But this Halloween, he was dressed in his normal guiding outfit: a fleece, jeans, and Vans skateboarding shoes.

We took off from Staten Island at around seven A.M. and headed for Jamaica Bay, the huge marine refuge for fish and fowl that's directly in the flight path of airplanes taking off and landing at JFK. We motored by the subsistence fishermen on the Canarsie Pier, all of whom gazed longingly at his boat, which seemed to promise access to fish just beyond the reach of their casts. The gathering of buildings in lower Manhattan—minus their huge twins, of course—was shrouded in fog in the near distance. No matter how you feel about urbanity—and I'm still on the fence—it's hard not to marvel at the majesty of its architecture, especially at this near distance. It's the feeling a knight must have had when ascending a hill for a first glimpse of a medieval castle.

We stopped near a bridge in Jamaica Bay when we saw working birds. The adrenaline of the city—that needle shot straight into the veins—is still very much present on the water in New York Harbor. Freighters and tugboats passed nearby. An aboveground subway snaked through the wind-whipped trees and shrubs of Far Rockaway. Helicopters buzzed overhead. The landing-gear screech of an incoming Qatar Airways 747 soaked up all noise not its own. On the water, the birds were going nuts. Bluefish were hitting everywhere, but they were doing so in pairs and singles and not in big voracious mobs, which somehow made them seem less menacing and more interesting, like the difference between cat burglars and arsonists.

Part of the adrenaline came from buck fever. With the fish feeding all around me, I couldn't figure out which one to cast to, so I tried in vain to cast to them all. As Captain Frank nudged the nose of the boat into the mayhem, he barked directions from the cockpit: "One o'clock. Now three o'clock. Eleven, eleven!! This is fucking awesome!" I felt like I'd accidentally wandered into a green-lighted intersection of Broadway and 42nd at rush hour. One of my casts hit the boat's antenna and broke off the fly. On one drift, I lost the entire fly line when I somehow wrapped it around the propeller.

Then I chilled. I finally got a cast near one duo that was busy chopping up a gathering of peanut bunker. One fish veered away from the assault, followed my fly like a bonefish, then inhaled it. "Fuck yes!" Captain Frank yelled, his dropped cigar hissing in the water. He netted the ten-pound blue and slapped my back with a big paw. I realized at that moment that I'd lived in this city for nearly a decade. It hit me that Captain Frank was a big reason why. This never wears off for him. He's ebullient, evangelical, frothing at the mouth, in love with the briny air, the boat, the cacophony of the harbor, the fish, the fishing, the company. He's more into it than anyone I know.

2008

3

Shark Bait

On a windy, overcast autumn day in Montauk, New York—the easternmost part of Long Island—I don a full-body, seven-millimeter wetsuit and flippers, and effectively put my life in the hands of a man who seems to have little regard for his own.

Paul Melnyk—a burly fifty-three-year-old who has Jack Nicholson's gravelly voice and the same raffish tilt to the eyebrows—is the creator of a discipline of extreme fishing known as "skishing," in which the practitioner swims in the open ocean while fishing. Melnyk, a cabinetmaker by day, calls himself the "skishin' magician," and boasts that the word "skishing" is now found in an online dictionary. "It's actually swim-fishing," he says. "But 'swishing' just didn't sound right to me."

Melnyk and I find an open slot among the crowd of surfcasters on the beach and duckwalk backward into the rough sea. We fall in and then kick on our backs hard for fifty yards to get out of the breaking waves that shoot briny water up my nose. When we are a hundred yards from shore, we stop swimming, caught—by design—in a fast-moving, northwesterly riptide, buoyed by our thick wetsuits. This is where the fish are. With a long cast by Melnyk at the crest of a four-foot wave, we are officially skishing.

It's oddly serene in the middle of the ocean. We are well out of reach of the beach fishers. The thunder of breaking waves is a distant rumble. The half-dozen charter boats chasing schools of fish are another two hundred yards or so out from us. This is Melnyk's zone. "It's a stealthy way to fish," he says. "The fish think you're just a log or something." We bob in the waves. Striped bass crash bait near us. Hovering birds overhead occasionally swoop down to pick through the carnage.

It's almost enough to make you forget the dangers, first and foremost drowning. Melnyk says first-time skishers often panic and have to be taken back to shore. A strong-enough riptide can send you flying past the tip of Montauk, next stop southern Europe. A few years ago a man skishing at night got caught in a strong rip, hooked a rock with his lure and spent a harrowing few hours holding onto his rod before being rescued by a boat.

Melnyk discovered skishing one day by accident, when, fishing from a rock, he was pulled into the ocean by a forty-pound fish. "I panicked at first, then I enjoyed it," he says. Likewise, there's always the chance a skisher will catch something so big and powerful that he finds himself doing some impromptu face-first skiing.

Then there are the sharks.

While Montauk is one of the world's premier destinations for striped bass, it's equally famous as a shark hot spot. The late Montauk fishing captain Frank Mundus, who claimed to be the inspiration for the shark-hunting character Quint in *Jaws*, caught great whites weighing 4,500 and 3,427 pounds. (He also penned the literary classic *Fifty Years a Hooker.*) Says Melnyk: "I've seen fins and been bumped by them. But they don't mess with me because I show no fear. I'm not afraid of dying."

Before I have time to let that statement sink in, Melnyk rears back with his rod and hooks into a striped bass. The fish jerks him forward just a bit, but he quickly regains control and reels it in. It's not a big bass—eight pounds or so; he's caught stripers up to fifty pounds while skishing—but Melnyk lets out a howl nonetheless and holds the fish up so the fishless surfcasters witness his success. Then he kisses the fish on the lips and flings it high in the air, an act meant to incense the surfcasters.

SHARK BAIT

Battle lines have been drawn. Melnyk has it in for the surfcasters, whom he refers to as "the billion morons on the shore." He only went whole hog into skishing in 1995, after being kicked out of a surfcasting tournament for swimming out to a rock to fish. "I really do this to spite those shore guys," he says. "I always wanted to be notorious for something." He's succeeded.

Melnyk and I start in for shore just before reaching the invisible line drawn out from the Montauk lighthouse, where the riptide can get unbearably strong. He has to make his six P.M. choral practice (he's a baritone). We emerge from the water like two sea monsters. He pulls down the top of his wetsuit, revealing a tattoo covering his entire right shoulder: a skeleton catching a striped bass. We pass a surfcaster, who stares at Melnyk, jaws agape like a hooked striper. "You ain't all there, are you?" says the surfcaster. Melnyk just grins.

2008

4

The Legend of Lefty

When it comes to Lefty Kreh, one must start with the cast. The slinging of a fly line is the essential act of fly-fishing, its biomechanical heart . . . and its single most significant barrier to entry. Kreh is one of the art's true grand masters, its greatest innovator, and its most prolific teacher. Though there are vastly more important gifts that Kreh has bestowed upon the sport over seven decades, it is primarily because of the cast that he is the most well-known fly fisherman in history, "the sport's Babe Ruth, but even bigger," as his friend and fellow fly-fishing icon, Flip Pallot, describes him. Unfortunately for Kreh and me, the cast we will begin with here is mine.

It is a cool spring day in Cockeysville, Maryland, and Kreh is driving his Toyota 4Runner through the town's gridded streets, carefully maintaining the speed limit. His left arm is comfortably placed on a homemade foam armrest fit into the driver's side door. On the top of his car, an orange fishing float that he's attached to the antenna bobs in the wind. "It sure as hell makes it easier to find this car in a crowded parking lot," he says by way of explanation.

We pass modest ranch houses, like the one Kreh lives in, and strips of stores. When Kreh moved here four decades ago, most of the area was still farmland. It is now a suburb, subsumed by the city of Baltimore. Kreh is wearing his hallmark hat, the "upper-downer," so named because of its side flaps, which he can pull down over his ears. The hat covers his bald spot, which Kreh calls "a solar panel for a love machine," one of his many go-to one-liners. The cloudy sky spits sporadic raindrops.

We pull into a little town park, which contains a small pond. Kreh hands me a rod. He recently celebrated his ninetieth birthday. For the most part, he appears and acts like a man much younger. He's never had to wear a hearing aid, nor does he need eyeglasses. His nine decades on earth have exacted some tolls, though. He's had a mild stroke, a heart attack, parts of his intestine removed, cataracts, and various serious knee problems. As he walks ahead of me, he teeters a bit, like an ocean buoy.

We come to a spot on the pond, maybe ten yards long, that's devoid of the knee-high grasses rimming the rest of the shoreline. "I keep this clear with a hand scythe," Kreh says. There's a faltering little waterspout in the middle of the pond. This is decidedly not the pastoral River Test in England, or some endless empty bonefish flat in Andros. But it is, appropriately, the place where Kreh has taken everyone, from the English gentry to elementary school janitors, to teach them to cast a fly rod better. To break down that barrier.

We rig up. "Let me see what you've got," he says. I am both nervous and excited to cast in front of the legend. I first picked up a fly rod when I was eight. Over the subsequent decades, I have cast them rather obsessively, and have long held the belief that I am reasonably proficient at it. That is, until now.

I take a few false casts and throw out some line.

"Did you look at your back cast?" Kreh asks.

"No," I meekly reply. It's another one of his go-tos, so I know the forthcoming punch line. That doesn't make it sting any less, though.

"Well, it's a good thing because it's ugly as hell," he says, then snorts, a tic of his that acts almost as a means of punctuation.

THE LEGEND OF LEFTY

Kreh has me do a double haul and then a few roll casts. "Okay, that's enough," he says. He trundles over and looks at me with his expressive eyes, which are the color of Bahamian blue holes. They convey his kindness and acuity and, occasionally, as I would learn later, a deep sadness. "We're going to make you better at this," he says, breaking into a wide grin that puffs up his cheeks and reveals a gap in his front teeth.

And then Kreh, who is almost a half century older than I am and, at five seven, nearly a foot shorter, effortlessly throws out the entire fly line, something many hardcore fly fishermen only dream of doing.

My problem—which I apparently share with many fly fishermen—is that I am stuck in the old "10 o'clock to 2 o'clock" casting method that's been taught for centuries. "Clocks are great for telling time, but they have nothing to do with fly-casting," Kreh says. I also move my wrist, lift my elbow, and keep my torso static. Kreh patiently works with me, at times holding me around the waist and casting with me. It takes an hour, but I eventually start to throw line farther than I ever have in my life.

We are at lunch, in a little café on a busy street in Cockeysville. Kreh orders the fried flounder and french fries, both "well done." He is notorious for a few abiding habits. One, of course, is the one-liners and the snorts that accompany them. Another is his nap, which he takes every day, no matter where he is. "Middle of the day, we'll be fishing and he'll say, 'Time for a nap' and lie on the bottom of the boat and just go out," says Oliver White, a fishing lodge owner who has fished with Kreh many times. "Twenty minutes later, he'll wake up and get right back at it."

His diet, too, is an object of fascination among those who know him. "He eats like a barbarian," says his friend Paul Bruun, the writer. Kreh likes his steak burned until it resembles a piece of charcoal. He brings Great Grains cereal and peanut butter and crackers with him on fishing trips so he can avoid unreliable lodge meals. He does not like vegetables, and will not tolerate "more than three different colors on my plate," he says.

At the café, he expounds a bit on the mechanics of the cast, using a very crisp french fry as a prop. "You don't actually cast a fly line," he says. "You unroll it like the treads on a tank."

Soon, though, he begins to talk about his life, in and out of fishing. Two men take the table next to ours. "That's Lefty Kreh," one of them whispers. They sit in silence throughout their lunch, shooting occasional furtive glances at our table, and listen as Kreh tells stories about his service in World War II, his exposure to a deadly biological weapon, his beloved wife, and his near excommunication from the world of fly-fishing.

Casting a fly rod, it becomes apparent, is just one part of the life of Lefty Kreh.

⊷

Bernard Victor Kreh was born in 1925, in Frederick, Maryland, some fifty miles west of Baltimore. In 1932, in the depth of the Depression, his father, a brickmason, was accidentally kicked in the chest during a basketball game and died.

Kreh, then six and the eldest of four children, became the man of the house. His family went on government relief (later known as welfare). Kreh was in charge of picking up sacks of flour and cornmeal from the government warehouse and pulling them home in a wagon. The sacks all had the word RELIEF printed prominently on their sides, which prompted merciless teasing from the other kids in town. "Everybody was poor back then, but we were really poor," he says. "We didn't have enough money to buy a mosquito underpants."

Kreh spent his free time tramping through the nearby woods and waters, hunting and fishing. "That's what we did back then," he says. "There were no posted signs or anything like that." He caught stringers of catfish and sold them for ten cents a pound, giving most of the money to his mother and then using whatever was left to buy his own clothes.

In school, he played baseball and basketball. He had good hand-eye coordination, was ambidextrous, and says he could see 180 degrees in his

THE LEGEND OF LEFTY

peripheral vision, traits that would come in handy later in his life. His friends nicknamed him "Lefty" for his ability to dribble a basketball with his left hand. (Many years ago, Kreh tore the biceps in his left arm while flipping a mattress. He's cast with his right hand ever since.)

After high school, Kreh enlisted in the US Army and became a member of the 69th Infantry Division in World War II. He arrived in Europe in late 1944 as the Allies were advancing across France and Belgium, headed for what would become known as the Battle of the Bulge, the catastrophic clash (with some ninety thousand American casualties) that took place regrettably late in the war. Kreh was, at various times, a forward observer, the lanyard puller on a howitzer, and a foot soldier.

Only now, Kreh says, can he comfortably talk about what he saw in the war. There were the everyday miseries, like spending freezing nights in a slit trench and waking up with a pancake of ice on his backside. There was the constant barrage of "Screaming Mimis," the German artillery rockets that contained horseshoes, chains, and other bits of flesh-tearing metal shrapnel. One day, an officer standing right in front of Kreh was hit by something and cleanly decapitated. Kreh was part of a group of soldiers who liberated a concentration camp that had only a hundred or so severely emaciated survivors. His one fond memory of the war: one morning, after his division had lived for weeks on cold rations, Allied planes swooped in low and dropped canisters containing hot syrup and pancakes. "We rolled them up and ate them like hot dogs," Kreh says.

In early 1945, Kreh's 69th Infantry Division met the Russian army at the Elbe River, and the war in Europe was effectively over. Kreh was sent home for a thirty-day furlough before he was supposed to be shipped to fight in the Pacific theater. "Then Truman dropped his bombs," he says.

Back home, Kreh found a job at Fort Detrick, the center for the United States' biological warfare program. One of his tasks was to don a protective plastic suit and scrape mud-like anthrax off cylinder walls so it could be processed for the site's scientists. The job wasn't glamorous, but the shift hours gave him plenty of time to hunt and fish.

One morning, Kreh remembers, he woke up feeling horrible. His right arm had turned black. Apparently, a small tear in his protective suit had exposed him to anthrax. For a month, he was kept alone in a small glass room for treatment. He would discover only later that scientists had extracted some of his blood to create a more virulent strain of anthrax, which they named BVK-1, using Kreh's initials.*

While working at Fort Detrick, Kreh began to make a name for himself as a local fisherman, especially when it came to smallmouth bass, which remain his favorite freshwater fish. (Bonefish are his favorite in the salt.) In 1947 an outdoor writer of some renown named Joe Brooks asked to fish with Kreh on the Potomac River. Brooks arrived with an Orvis Battenkill bamboo fly rod. "I'd never laid eyes on a fly rod before that," says Kreh, who was then strictly a plug caster and spin fisherman. He was mesmerized watching Brooks fish. The next day, Kreh drove to Baltimore and bought a South Bend fiberglass fly rod and a Pflueger Medalist reel and, within months, became an expert caster.

Kreh leveraged that into invitations to exhibitions. He dazzled crowds by throwing an entire fly line with just his hand and by casting, now with a rod, and knocking cigarettes out of the mouths of comely young women from eighty feet away. Sometime later he took an old carp-fishing friend who was skeptical about fly-fishing to a river to show him how it was done. Kreh put on a display, casting two, then four, then eight rods (held between his fingers) at the same time. He turned to his friend and said, "Well, whaddya think?"

His friend just looked at him. "It ain't worth a shit. You ain't caught anything yet."

The showmanship began to leave Kreh feeling unfulfilled. In the mid-1950s, he says, "I quit all the hotdogging and decided it was better to actually teach people."

---

* The comic-book geek in me can't help but wonder if this is the moment—akin to Peter Parker's getting bitten by the radioactive spider—when Kreh developed his superpowers as a fly fisherman, powers that would come into full bloom just a short while later.

THE LEGEND OF LEFTY

The exhibitions became places where Kreh shared his knowledge instead of flaunting it. He tirelessly worked with anyone—especially young children—who wanted to learn about rigging knots, tying flies, and casting. "I've seen his casting demonstration a hundred times, but I still watch," says Tom Rosenbauer, the marketing head at Orvis. "I learn something new every time." Kreh, a classic extrovert, was made for entertaining. "I've been with him when he isn't feeling well, then he gets around a group of people and starts talking fishing and he gets energy," says Ted Juracsik, a friend and founder of the Tibor Reel company. The exhibitions benefited Kreh as well. "I learn from everybody," he says. "People ask me something and I look for the answer. A lot of times you would never look for the answer unless you have a question. And everything I do is always subject to change."

Exhibitions are also where Kreh has unleashed some of his best quips. Once, when telling a story about a particularly productive lagoon in Cuba, he said, "I cast my fly in there and it wasn't coming out. It was like rolling a wine bottle into a jail cell." He told the crowds he once dated a girl so ugly "that the tide wouldn't take her out." He talked about a man he knew who was "so lazy that he married a pregnant woman." Kreh is among the last of the great politically incorrect storytellers, something he gets away with because his general demeanor suggests he means no harm. Once, while doing a presentation in Pennsylvania, his projector broke. To kill time, Kreh told the audience he'd start telling some Polish jokes. Some of the men present stood and told Kreh they, in fact, were Polish. "That's all right, fellas," Kreh replied. "I'll tell them nice and slow so you can understand." The men all laughed.

Kreh also wrote articles—all how-to ("I don't do that fancy stuff," he says)—for regional and national publications, sometimes churning out four or five pieces a week. Over the years, he's had outdoor columns in the *Baltimore Sun* and *Fly Fisherman* and *Outdoor Life* magazines, among others. He began writing books as well. *Practical Fishing and Boating Knots* has reportedly sold more than three hundred thousand copies. If one takes into account the additional thirty books Kreh has written, and the countless magazine and newspaper articles he's penned over the

24 RIVERS ALWAYS REACH THE SEA

last sixty years, it's very likely that he is the most widely read angling writer in history.

To gather material, Kreh traveled the world. He fished in New Guinea for a species of bass nicknamed the River Rambo. He went to Cuba in 1960 to write about Ernest Hemingway's white marlin tournament, fishing with Fidel Castro one day ("He talked about the future of the country, but never mentioned the word *communism*," Kreh says) and aboard *Pilar* with Hemingway for two days. (Castro won the tournament, legitimately as far as Kreh could tell.) Kreh traveled to Australia, New Zealand, France, England, South America, and Central America. He cast a line in all fifty states in America. Along the way, he helped open new fly-fishing frontiers. He extolled the virtues of barramundi fishing in Australia. He spread the word about fishing for striped bass on the flats in the Northeast. "It was here, but no one paid much attention until Lefty started to talk about it," says Paul Dixon, a guide in Long Island, New York. Kreh did the same thing for false albacore in North Carolina. He also helped kickstart the targeting of new fly rod species, such as muskellunge and carp.

In the late 1950s, Kreh created one of the most popular flies in the sport's history, the Lefty's Deceiver. The inveterate tinkerer devised it, of course, while looking for an answer to a question. Traditional streamer flies at the time often fouled, the feathers wrapping around the hook. Kreh solved that problem by adding a hair collar that surrounded the wing of the fly and kept it off the hook. "I really thought it was just a passing thing when I made it, but it caught on," he says. In 1991, the US Postal Service put the Lefty's Deceiver on a stamp.

From 1964 to 1972 (when he moved back to Maryland), Kreh lived in South Florida and ran the Miami Metropolitan Fishing Tournament, a sixteen-week event that attracted people from all over the world. Kreh was the hub of all activity, connecting guides and clients and writers and manufacturers. South Florida was then in the vanguard of saltwater fly-fishing and home to angling pioneers such as Pallot, Stu Apte, Chico Fernandez, Jimmie Albright, George Hommell, and Ted Williams. There, Kreh bore witness to, and took an

THE LEGEND OF LEFTY

active role in, many of the lasting innovations in the sport—in knots, casting, flies, and boats.

But it was never just about the fish and the fishing for Kreh. "There are literally thousands of people who will tell you that they are friends of Lefty's, which is a phenomenal occurrence," Pallot says. Says Kreh, "I like to see people succeed." In the late 1980s, he helped a young flytier named Bob Popovics gain acceptance for his new breed of flies—like the invaluable Surf Candy—which many fly fishermen had deemed too radical because they utilized epoxies and monofilament. Around the same time, a man named Bob Clouser showed Kreh a new fly he'd designed, which had weighted eyes. The fly-fishing cognoscenti dismissed his fly as merely a spin caster's jig. But Kreh went to bat for Clouser, and his fly, the Clouser Minnow, is now one of the most popular flies in the world. "Lefty never blew out another person's candle to make his own burn brighter," Clouser says. "He taught me a lot. How to cast. How to act."

Kreh has also long been an ardent supporter of women in fly-fishing. "They're smarter and more perceptive than men," he says. When Candus Thomson became the outdoor columnist at the *Baltimore Sun*—Kreh's former gig—she faced some serious chauvinism. "There were a lot of dudes out there who didn't want me to have the job and didn't think I could do it," she says. "Lefty told me that if anyone messed with me, they were messing with him." Sarah Gardner, a well-respected guide in North Carolina, says Kreh encouraged her early on. "He gave me the confidence to do this. I owe him everything."

The writings, exhibitions, and instruction, and his overall ambassadorship, effectively turned Kreh into modern fly-fishing's gospel spreader. He was in the right place at the right time, teaching and preaching just as an entire generation of men like him were returning from a horrific war. "Flyfishing was like a type of therapy for all of us," he says. He was a common man, intensely practical, helping other common men and women enter a sport that, at that time, was particularly elitist and somewhat stunted by orthodoxy. "He's always brought an earthiness and simplicity to something that a lot of people make a very complex activity," says Nick Lyons, a friend and the publisher of many of Kreh's books.

At one point, however, that practicality briefly turned the sport's Apostle Paul into one of fly-fishing's greatest apostates.

With the exception of one quick casting lesson from Joe Brooks ("the old 10-to-2 method, of course," Kreh says), he had never been "taught" to cast, and thus developed his own style. Kreh's cast was predicated on getting out as much line as possible and casting effectively—and effortlessly—in windy conditions. "I learned early on that the longer your fly was in the water, the better the chance you had at catching fish," he says. His method—the longer, flatter backstroke, the moving of the caster's torso—flew directly in the face of centuries of fly-casting instruction. As such, many of the old guard did not like it very much.

In March 1965, Kreh went public with his new way of casting in an article published in *Outdoor Life*. It turned out to be the fly-fishing equivalent of Martin Luther's posting of the Ninety-five Theses. Irate letters poured into the magazine's offices. Subscriptions were canceled. Kreh heard the criticism to his face. The English, it seemed, were the most perturbed by his attack on fly-fishing's established customs. When Kreh visited England one year, some lords confronted him and asked if his cast could indeed get the fly out farther. "I said, 'Is a bullfrog waterproof?'" Kreh says. "They had no idea what a bullfrog was."

The skeptical men asked him to prove it. They took Kreh to a swimming pool. Kreh attached a set of heavy hotel keys to his fly line and proceeded to cast the rig effortlessly. The lords turned red in the face. "I've always questioned everything, especially the absolutes," Kreh says.

In the end, Kreh's geniality, talent, and unceasing search for a better way to do things would quiet the maelstrom his new teachings caused, and they would become accepted as an integral part of the sport's canon. As one of Kreh's friends once said about his place within the elitist fly-fishing world: "He's a smart country boy in a world of fast-talking snobs. They never stood a chance."

THE LEGEND OF LEFTY   27

After lunch, Kreh and I go back to his impeccably tidy house. In the basement, he has dozens of reels, all arranged by size in perfect rows on a wall. At least forty fly rods, in cases, are neatly hung on an adjacent wall. On nearby shelves sit stacks of Ziploc bags, trash bags, and Great Grains cereal. I point to what looks like a mini Costco on his shelves, and he merely shrugs. "I'm a child of the Depression," he says.

In the living room, there's a mount of a hundred-pound tarpon, a species he says he has "no more desire to catch" because of the long and brutish fight they put up. On the second floor, in Kreh's fly-tying room, there is not a single speck of fur or feather on the floor. Hundreds of hooks in all different sizes, feathers, and weighted barbell fly eyes are stacked in meticulously marked boxes on the shelves. Stuck on his fly-tying vise is a giant white streamer fly that looks nearly big enough to qualify as a family pet. Across the hallway is Kreh's writing office, adorned with photos of fish on the walls and a large-screen computer on his desk, one of two he owns. (Kreh has long been an early adopter of technology.)

Amid all the fly-fishing mementos in prominent spots around his house are photos of Kreh's wife Evelyn, whom he called "Ev." Kreh and Ev were married for sixty-six years. "We had the greatest marriage of anyone I know," he says. He met the pretty blond one night at a theater after the war. They married a year later and had two children. Ev encouraged Kreh's life in fly-fishing. When he left for trips, he would sometimes leave behind Hershey's Kisses for every day he was gone, each wrapped in a little homemade love note.

In 2009, Ev had a debilitating stroke and developed dementia. "I looked after her for two years," Kreh says, his eyes beginning to mist. "I wanted to take care of my lady myself." Ev died in 2011. Kreh, then eighty-six, spiraled downward rapidly. "He was in rough shape then, physically and mentally," says Yvon Chouinard, the founder of Patagonia, who has known him for thirty years. Kreh says he sat around the house for a few months feeling sorry for himself. "Then one day I realized how fortunate I had been," he says. "I still think about her every day."

Though Kreh has not dated anyone since Ev's death, a particularly randy thirtysomething fly-fishing groupie tried to change that a few years ago. One day, she accosted him at a fishing camp and demanded he rendezvous with her in an Airstream trailer after fishing. Taken aback, Kreh cut his fishing day short and persuaded a friend at the camp to drive him to the airport before the appointed hour. As they hustled off, Kreh told his friend the reason behind his hasty departure. The friend pretended to turn the car around and take him back to camp. "He thought he was pretty funny," Kreh says.

Kreh rebounded from Ev's death by throwing himself completely into fly-fishing. He follows a travel schedule that would exhaust someone half his age. When I met with him, he was just back from the Bahamas. After three days at home, catching up on his emails and bills, he was off to Dallas to shoot a film. His itinerary for the next few months included a return to the Bahamas and fishing trips in Ontario, Wisconsin, Maine, Louisiana, Montana, and Idaho. In recent years, his troublesome knees have slowed him down on the water. He can no longer stand in a flats boat. Still, he's had some memorable moments. Once, when fishing with Ted Juracsik in the Keys, he broke his rod on his first cast. He fished the rest of the day with just the tip of the rod and landed many redfish and juvenile tarpon in an area Juracsik has since named Broken Rod Bay. Aaron Adams, the head scientist at the Bonefish & Tarpon Trust, remembers a day on the water in the Bahamas when Kreh was sitting on an ice chest in the bow of the boat, deep in a conversation with the writer Thomas McGuane. "The guide spotted a bonefish and told Lefty, 'Twelve o'clock, a hundred feet.' Lefty turned, took two false casts, and nailed the fish," Adams says. "He had cataract surgery a few days later."

Though frustrated by his physical limitations, Kreh has not let them weigh him down. "I still really like to catch fish, but my greatest pleasure is to help people with their casting, and when they catch that bass or trout or bonefish, it's almost like I did."

THE LEGEND OF LEFTY

That spirit of generosity is at the heart of his remarkable life and the affection it has engendered. "I have to be careful here not to sound too excessive," says avid fly fisherman Tom Brokaw, who has gotten to know Kreh over the last decade. "But I've really come to love him." Perhaps Bob Clouser best sums up the general feeling that surrounds his longtime friend and mentor: "I wish he could live forever."

2015

5

Jamaica Bay

New York City's destiny was determined by its geography. It was once one of the most naturally bountiful and beautiful places in this country. You may not believe this, but it's true. Game (deer, elk, turkey, bear) was abundant. A great river to the west (the Hudson) and a tidal strait to the east (the East River) teemed with striped bass, sturgeon, shad, blackfish, fluke, weakfish, porgies, and bluefish. Anadromous brook trout made spawning runs up freshwater spring creeks that sluiced through the hilly, grassy land (Brooklyn, my home for the last twelve years, was named after Breuckelen, a town in the Netherlands famous for its brooks). The weather was temperate, with a robust four seasons. The area was protected from the ocean's fury by a land barrier that would later become known as Long Island.

In other words, New York City was once pretty much a perfect human habitat, which is the reason we are now here in such stupendously unnatural numbers and have perverted nature so appallingly. The explorers Giovanni da Verrazzano and Henry Hudson witnessed this lost world while unwittingly initiating its fall. What they saw—that state of natural grace—is so long gone, so deeply repressed and paved over, it's as if it never existed.

There is, however, at least one spot where it can be reached, in a sense.

It's late fall, 4:30 A.M., and I'm wading in Jamaica Bay, named for the Lenape word *yemecah*, which means "place of the beaver." I'm alone. While anonymity is easy to achieve in New York City, solitude is not. But it is possible to find out here this early in the morning.

The herring are in. Their arrival portends the end of the fall run. But it goes out with a bang. The biggest stripers, following the herring, form the rear guard of the mass migration south.

When I first moved to the city, I used to pack my fishing gear as compactly as I could and take the A train to its terminus in the Rockaways, riding in the wee hours of the morning with the dozing homeless, the fidgety addicts, and the club-goers with their dilated pupils. On the ride home my pack dripped seawater from the waders within it. I now have a car. It's a pain in the ass to keep in the city. It's worth it for this alone.

I make a cast with a heavily dressed fly. In the distance, lights halo the tallest buildings in Manhattan. The wind is out of the west, against the outgoing tide, which makes for a nice drift. On my third cast, I get a solid take but quickly lose the fish. There is a drop-off here filled with some rocks from a jetty that was abandoned long ago. The bait like the structure and, thus, so do the stripers. I am not too far from the spot where Henry Hudson anchored the *Half Moon* in September (albie season!) 1609, gazed at the inlet leading into Jamaica Bay, and mistakenly believed it to be the boca of a major river.

Something in the water bumps against my leg. It startles me. I've often wondered if I was ever going to run across a facedown Lorenzo or Rocco from Canarsie—a floater—who got on the wrong side of a bad deal. I am relieved to discover it is just a coconut. I learn later that there has been a plague of coconuts in the water this fall. The Hindus in Queens have been using Jamaica Bay as a proxy for the Ganges. Floating coconuts are apparently part of a purifying religious ceremony.

JAMAICA BAY

There is no escaping Man and his detritus in Jamaica Bay. It is after all, located within the boroughs of Queens and Brooklyn, and touched by a sliver of Long Island's Nassau County (combined population: more than six million people). Since Hudson's time, 75 percent of the bay's marshlands have been filled in. The shoreline consists of some parkland, but is also bordered by busy roads, tightly arrayed houses, a derelict former military airport, and even an old dump that bulges under newly planted native grasses. JFK Airport, which handles an astounding four hundred thousand flights a year, dominates the eastern end.

Over the years, I've spotted a half-dozen Coney Island Whitefish (read: condoms) floating by, a few of those robin's-egg blue tampon applicators, and various submerged plastic bags, which are always unnervingly animated by the current. After big storms, I've seen all sorts of unsavory things wash up on the beach: beer bottles, syringes, deflated balloons, candy wrappers, a refrigerator, part of a dock, a dead squirrel.

Yet nature is unrelenting. Much of the ten thousand acres of Jamaica Bay is wildlife refuge and, at times, when deep in the marsh grasses or kayaking around an undeveloped island or wading in the dark, you can feel "out there." The bay hosts three hundred and thirty different species of migratory and nonmigratory birds. Red-tailed hawks fly methodical circles over the dunes. Ring-necked pheasants scoot through the switch grass. In the last two winters, I've spotted five majestic snowy owls. Thousands of butterflies and horseshoe crabs migrate through each year. Diamondback terrapins inching their way across the tarmacs at JFK have brought plane traffic to an abrupt halt on numerous occasions.

And, oh yes, there are fish. Jamaica Bay fishes well for nearly eight months of the year. It is thick with stripers and blues from the spring through the late fall. There are stable numbers of weakfish. Bonito drop in for a bit during some summers. False albacore wreak their havoc in the inlet in September and October.

I've fished the bay from a boat with captains Frank Crescitelli, John McMurray, and Brendan McCarthy. On the mudflats in the spring, a Gurgler can take a striper, a blue, or a weakfish. The stripers feeding on grass shrimp near the islands sometimes look like trout bumping nymphs just under the water's surface. In the early summer, it is possible to sight-fish big cruisers in the shallows of the northwest portion of the bay near the Belt Parkway.

One of the better spots in the bay is a borrow pit that was dredged to help create the runways at JFK. There, a cat-and-mouse game is played with the airport security guys in boats, who will flick on their blue lights and chase you away when they deem you too close. The wiliest fishing captains have learned how to dart in and out, nipping around the edges while throwing sink tips down deep for twenty pounders. This close to the airport, one must get accustomed to the incoming and outgoing planes which create a deafening, almost time-stopping sound.

I like boats, but most of my fishing in Jamaica Bay is done—as it is this morning—from the shore.

The wind is picking up. I keep casting into the dropping tide, probing, as it turns out, in vain. The solitude ends with the breaking of dawn. The boats—guides, commercial guys, poachers—start making their way toward the ocean. Lights inside nearby houses flick on. The city is stirring.

Two hours after I started, I reel up and head back to my car, fishless. It's no matter. Jamaica Bay is one of the main reasons I still live here. The fish aren't the only thing I'm after.

2015

6

My Spot, Burned

Editor's note: Some of the names in this story have been changed to protect the guilty.

L et me tell you a little bit about my spot. I cannot tell you the name. It would be the biggest spot burn in the history of burning spots, immediately qualifying for the spot burn Hall of Fame, no five-year waiting period required. You see, my spot is just a dozen or so miles outside the limits of the nation's most populous city, that one of eight million stories. It's on a long island crammed with another eight million folks. That's sixteen million people, man. If even .00001 percent of them showed up at my spot, it would be ruinous. So I won't tell you the name, or even the exact location. But I will tell you a little bit about it.

My spot is not too far from a major metropolitan airport. Fishermen frequently shade their eyes to glance up at the piscine underbellies of incoming 747s. You can see my spot from your window seat when you fly in from the north, from Boston or Montreal. It is on a peninsula, which means you have a daily choice: inside or out. It has a cut inlet deep and busy with boats. There are a few short jetties present, constructed of slick, black, algae-covered boulders. It fishes eight months of the year. It's a pretty good spot to find a striper or blue or false albacore or weakfish. There are sea robins there, too.

The spot is certainly no secret; there may be no such a thing around these parts. But let's still refrain from naming it, okay?

Most of the fishermen there are spin guys. Bait-and-lure-chuckers. They think fly fishermen are weird. There is a group of Asians, known on the beach as "the Chinese Navy," who like to fish at the tip of one of the jetties. They often take big rogue-ish waves right in the kisser, but remain insensate. There are usually a handful of Russians around. In the heat of the summer they sometimes come over on Jet Skis from an unknown location. Often they are accompanied by very young-looking women wearing wispy bikinis. On the Jet Skis, these women cling to their pilots, wrapping skinny arms and legs around ballooned bellies.

There is one Orthodox Jewish man who always removes his shoes in the parking lot and fishes barefoot, no matter the temperature—I've seen him standing on a jetty on a very brisk day in late October. This seems like something religious, an act of purification. He wears a ball cap with a large Nike swoosh emblazoned on the front. It all seems to work for him. He catches fish.

Then there are the fly fishermen. There are only four of us, maybe five. This place is a secret we grip tightly and jealously. We all laugh at how often we find ourselves at parties, at gatherings, bursting with the urge to tell everyone we see about our good fortune, to grab them one by one by the lapels and say, "My God, man, you have no idea!" But our pact is sacred.

There is Rob, whose big white teeth, thin-but-slicked-back hair and pencil-thin dark gray mustache bring to mind a 1920s-era Hemingway. Rob is retired. He casts without any discernible plan or concentration, at least to the outsider's eye. But he seems awful happy just to be out there.

There is Neil. He's a hot-shit architect in the city. He's also a fishing vagabond. Though he likes it out here, beyond the city, best, he's not beholden to just this spot. He also fishes the city hard, knows all its haunts. He sometimes fishes, predawn, by the boat slips at the southern

MY SPOT, BURNED

tip of the city, where the homeless occasionally come to wail at the sea. In the spring, Neil wades the mudflats up by one of the baseball stadiums. He's fishy: he bagged a permit on his very first trip south.

Then there's the Loon. He's our ringleader. Everyone knows the Loon, even the spin guys. He's been at it for decades. When I first showed up here a few years ago, I was asked more than once, "You must know the Loon, right?" I didn't then, but I do now.

The Loon is as skinny as a pipe cleaner. He was a wrestler back in school and could still make weight even now in his sixties. He has a gray mustache and wears one of those floppy sun hats like Lefty does. He uses his entire body when he fishes. His casts seem to originate from his toes. He walks a bit like a heron, moving only his legs. One time I saw him lose an absolutely enormous striper, the biggest I'd ever seen on a fly rod. It came off after five minutes of battle. His body immediately contorted into a question mark. "Why?" it asked.

<hr />

The hurricane wrecked my spot. The indifferent sea that once created it gobbled it right back up. It left a new, temporary inlet. It wiped out all of the dunes. There is no more altitude to the sand on the peninsula, leaving it horribly vulnerable to the wind.

A month after the hurricane hit, I went out to my spot. It was very early in the morning. I will admit that I had my fly-fishing gear with me. It looked like something a war had left behind. Huge floodlights were everywhere, I guess to discourage looting. A few houses had been destroyed, leaving only crisscrossed rows of lumber or ashy heaps. Backhoes and dump trucks were parked in the fishermen's lots. Hand-painted signs were everywhere: CLEAN WATER; HAZARDOUS WASTE DISPOSAL AREA; GENERAL CONTRACTOR. CALL RONNIE: 516-XXX-XXXX. Cop cars idled on the desolate streets, their red and blue lights silently streaming across the night.

I pulled up to the one of those cars, slowly. There was a cop inside. He was out, head tilted back, mouth wide open. The posture of the sleep-deprived. I left him alone. I parked by the beach and walked to the water. Its waves were the only thing that looked familiar.

This was usually *the* prime time in these parts. The big girls showed about now, with the herring and the gannets. I couldn't bring myself to fish, for what happened to be entirely selfish reasons. There was misery all around me. I wouldn't have felt comfortable being spotted casting a line when the sun eventually raised the curtain of darkness. I didn't want to feel the guilt. So I left. I called the Loon. I emailed Neil. We were all thinking now.

2013

7

First Tarpon

We skid turns through the labyrinth of backcountry mangroves. A few stars are visible in the pale early morning light, but they are fading, soon to be hidden again. I'm sitting in the back of the skiff next to Steve Huff, who holds the tiller under his armpit. He is a man completely within his element.

As the scenery in the Everglades—the green vegetation on the banks, the blue sky and water—blends together, I can't help but voice the clichéd thought:

How in the hell would I get out of here if you keeled over?

Huff's smile straightens out his white mustache.

You wouldn't.

I gaze at his hands for maybe the third time that morning. You might find this strange, but I can't help it. Stories are worn into those hands, maybe even Commandments. They are gnarled by calluses and deeply etched scars, parched by decades in the sun. They look like old mangroves, whited-out by the elements. They have handled world-record tarpon, bonefish, and permit. They have pushed boats with poles for thousands of miles across sand flats. They have built and rebuilt skiffs from the ground up, some of which are still in use even forty years later. They are the hands of a man who has never had an email address.

It is the spring of 2011, and I am on my first trip for tarpon. The weather is perfect, sun with no clouds, a light breeze. The tarpon are in, Huff says. I am a bit too jazzed. Sleep the night before had proven nearly impossible.

We come to a stop in the boca of a river, the engine cut, the wash *shooshing* against the stern. Huff tilts the motor, grabs the push pole, and climbs up on his platform. I stand and walk to the bow, fly rod in hand. My knees scrape against the raised casting platform that I feel a bit too clumsy to ascend just yet.

This boca is where Bloody Watson, the real-life murderer and outlaw fictionalized by Peter Matthiessen, once lived. Huff tells me this as he begins to pole the boat, slowly and deliberately, never taking his eyes off the water.

He spots a tarpon. It's lying there, near the surface, a serene six-foot beast at rest. My mind empties, swiftly. It's something we all seek to achieve, this purposeful clearing of the brain. Some find it via alcohol, drugs, sex, yoga. Some of us fish for it.

The fish is facing left. I cast there, tentatively, aiming for a spot maybe a foot in front of her nose. I instead land it on her head. The fish flushes, pushing a boat-sized wake. It's no problem, Huff says. There are more around. We find another one again within minutes, and I screw up that cast, too. Then we find another, and I blow it again.

A few tarpon roll in the distance.

That I am here on the water with Huff at all is a bit of a fluke. I had written a story about him the prior winter, and we'd spent some time in the boat together. We'd hit it off. But for decades, he has had a static list of fifteen people he fishes with each year. He once turned down a fishing request from George H. W. Bush. After one trip, a client gave

FIRST TARPON

him a condominium as a tip. But this week, as fortune had it, one of his regulars couldn't make his appointed trip and suggested I go in his stead. And here I am.

Huff describes tarpon as heroin. He has been, for decades, perhaps the world's foremost dealer in this fish drug. A prominent magazine once described him as "The Best Fishing Guide Alive." He is, some fifty-plus years into his career, a legend among legions of guides, their DiMaggio, still in his prime. He says his only job is to make an angler's dream come true. He plays the role of coach/mentor/psychologist, which all great guides must do, with aplomb. I have now blown three great shots at tarpon. By all rights, I should be a slobbering mess, fit for the funny farm. But I am not.

We're going to get one, he says.

I believe him.

Later in the day, I finally make a good cast, right in front of the bigger member of a brace of laid-up tarpon. I get no response from the fish but am buoyed by the act, like a golfer in the midst of a bad round who finally feels something click on one swing.

Right there, to the left!

I see it. A monster fish has gulped air and then remained floating near the water's surface. I make the cast immediately, without any thought, make one strip, and then feel a pull I will never forget. Before I can even process what's going on, the she-tarpon clears the water *behind* us.

Images of the moment come to me now, in bits and pieces. I see the water part when the fish bites the fly. I see Huff somehow duck his head under my fly line, avoiding a clotheslining as it slices through the air over him, tight as a guitar string.

Half an hour into the fight, I realize my face has been contorted into a rictus, the openmouthed grimace of the dead. I am pulling on the fish, trying to follow Huff's instructions. Yet I can't seem to get the upper hand. My back is numb, my shins and knees rubbed raw by the casting platform I'm leaning into. I understand at that moment why people say they sometimes give up while fighting a big tarpon, that it's easier to get a few jumps from one like this, then break it off and call it a day.

But I can't do that. This is my first.

She pulls the boat and its two occupants upriver a mile or so, to a mangrove-lined feeder creek barely big enough to fit us all. This is maybe where she grew up. I notice Huff has put on a pair of orange landing gloves. The fight has taken two hours. I am embarrassed, but not enough to stop. The fly line has begun to come apart, its coating stripped by submerged mangrove roots. Huff tells me that Billy Pate Jr. once fought a tarpon for more than twelve hours. Pate would have been a lousy fishing partner. I swear to myself that I will get better at this, someday.

She finally comes up, leading with her huge, prehistoric-looking mouth. Huff holds her for a moment and removes the fly. He moves her a bit in the water, reviving her. She shoots off with a kick of her tail. Huff removes his gloves to shake my hand.

Congratulations, says the dream-maker.

Waves of relief and exhaustion nearly bring me to my knees. My lower back throbs in pain. My shirt is soaked through with sweat, and I feel like puking from dehydration. My right hand is grotesquely stuck in a curl, as if still holding the rod handle.

I cannot wait to do it all over again.

2016

8

The Dream-Maker

It's early morning in Chokoloskee, Florida, and Steve Huff is slowly guiding us away from the dock. The bow of his Hell's Bay skiff is pointed toward the labyrinth of mangroves and buttonwoods that give shape to the mesmeric Everglades, where Huff spends nearly two hundred days a year. He's wearing a bandanna patterned with fish scales. It covers his sunburned nose and trimmed cotton-white mustache. His long arms dangle from a wiry, compact body that seems almost simian in its alertness and strength.

Then he guns the engine. As the boat planes quickly and easily, Huff lifts up his bandanna, revealing a wide smile.

"Do you feel that?" he yells to me over the engine's whine. "We're free."

Steve Huff is sixty-five. He has been a fishing guide for forty-three of those years, first in the Florida Keys and now in the Everglades City area, where he moved in 1996 with his bright-eyed wife, Patty. Huff's specialty is fishing the skinny saltwater flats for tarpon, bonefish, permit, and snook, and he has guided his clients to countless world-record fish. Last year he was inducted into the International Game Fish Association's Hall of Fame, which is the fishing world's Cooperstown. In his book,

A Passion for Tarpon, Andy Mill calls Huff "bar none, the best tarpon guide alive, the best there was and the best there ever will be." Marshall Cutchin, a former Keys guide and the editor and publisher of the fly-fishing website midcurrent.com, goes even further, calling him "the best guide who's ever lived, period."

This type of talk embarrasses Huff, who prefers to shower accolades on others. "Steve is a really humble guy," says Sandy Moret, who owns a fly shop in the Keys and has fished with Huff for three decades. For Huff, it's all pretty simple. "I'm just a fishing guide," he says. "My job is to make an angler's dream come true."

His own dreams are part of the equation. Guiding, at its essence, is a selfless endeavor, geared to the happiness and success of the paying customer, the "dream-making." But for Huff, there is the rush—of being on the water nearly every day and trying to figure out the puzzle presented by the tides, the wind, the clouds, the fish, and the angler's ability. The climax, that final puzzle piece, is the hooking and landing of the guided angler's targeted fish. Huff can't live without that rush.

<hr>

Huff was born and raised in Miami. When he was ten, his father gave him a spinning rod, the first piece of tackle he'd ever owned. His father left the next day. Huff would neither see nor speak to him again. "He was an alcoholic and a gambler," Huff says. "He probably died in a ditch somewhere."

Huff is unsentimental about the impact that his father's leaving might have had on his life. "I think we grow up to be whatever we were meant to be," he says. And anyway, with that fishing rod, his father provided him with the first tool for what would become his life's abiding passion. Huff took the rod, cast into a Miami canal, and caught a two-pound snook. "That was it," he says. "I was done." He biked all over the city, fishing in backyards and canals. One day he sneaked down a manhole in the middle of a causeway bridge. He cast a lure from a ladder and caught a twenty-seven-pound snook, to this day his largest. He knew then that he would be a guide someday.

THE DREAM-MAKER

While attending the University of Miami, Huff studied marine biology. When he graduated, he told his mother of his career plans. She was not pleased. "She told me that fishing guides were a bunch of drunks and bums and that I would never amount to anything," Huff says.

Still, she cosigned a bank loan so Huff could buy his first guide boat. He moved to the Keys, and on November 1, 1968, he took out his first client. "Poor bastard," Huff says. The day was windy and overcast and fishless. The guy never came back. "I had no clue what I was doing," Huff says. "I didn't even know what I didn't know."

But Huff was determined to figure it out. He poled for miles, into the teeth of twenty-five-knot headwinds. ("Best poler I've ever seen," Cutchin says.) He scouted and discovered new spots. He tied his own flies, designed his own boats, invented new fishing knots. He stayed out longer than anyone else, making the run back to the dock in complete darkness. He never gave up.

Within a few years, people who fished with him once never wanted to leave. "He's intense and he expects you to match that intensity," says one of his clients, the author Carl Hiaasen. "It makes you a better angler." Bill Hassett, a sporting goods store owner in St. Louis, Missouri, has fished with Huff for thirty-seven consecutive years. Lenny Berg, an ophthalmologist in Fort Pierce, Florida, has been with him for thirty-five years. Hiaasen is a relative newcomer, having fished with Huff for fifteen years. "I just feel fortunate that he let me on his boat," Hiaasen says, laughing.

Those who do fish with him tend to get greedy. The late Del Brown once booked Huff for fifty-five days one year to fish for permit in the Keys. Tom Evans, holder of sixteen world records, once locked him in from March 1 to June 15. Huff now has a list of about fifteen clients to whom he is intensely loyal (he turned down a trip with George H. W. Bush in favor of one of his already-booked regulars). He has taken on exactly one new client in the last twenty years.

His clients have become his closest friends. "When you're in a small boat together for ten to twelve hours a day, you quickly get past the small talk," Huff says. "You laugh and you cry together." One client constantly complained about his wife for years. Hoping to change the subject on the water one day, Huff bluntly told him he should divorce her. The man called a week later and told Huff he had filed divorce papers. "I said, 'You've got to be shitting me,'" Huff says.

As with all intense relationships, complications can arise. Huff no longer fishes with one of his longest-tenured clients. "One day I just told him what he was: a selfish prick," Huff says. The guy asked Huff why it took him so long to figure that out. To this day, the two still talk on the phone a few times a year, unable to completely disconnect. One of the saddest endings came with Del Brown, who posthumously still holds twelve world records. Huff and Brown had fished together since 1980. They were a perfect pair on the water, with matching intensity and drive. But one late afternoon in 2001, when Brown was eighty-three, Huff poled for an hour into the wind to get Brown in position to fish. Huff waited for Brown to hold up his end of the bargain and cast. But Brown put his rod down and told Huff he wanted to go in. Huff was wracked with heaving sobs as he ran the boat in. At the dock, he told Brown through tears that he could not fish with him anymore. "It was really my problem," Huff says. "Del was getting older and I just didn't want to admit it. It broke my heart." Brown died two years later.

Huff has witnessed many strange moments during his forty-three years on the water. An unhooked hundred-pound tarpon once leaped into his boat and hit a female client squarely in the chest. (On his boat the next year, she wore a flak jacket as a gag.) One year he was fishing with Tom Evans when Evans suddenly had to use the bathroom. As Evans hung off the back of the boat, he asked Huff to cast for a rolling tarpon. Huff did, and he hooked and landed a 186-pound tarpon, which would have been the world record. But Huff never submitted it to the International Game Fish Association (IGFA). "Tom wanted that record so badly," he says. A week later, Huff led Evans into a 177-pounder, which indeed did become the world record.

But perhaps the strangest thing happened with a man named Everett Watkins, who flew from California to fish with a friend who had set up a trip with Huff. Watkins, an obese man, hooked a 125-pound tarpon on one of his first casts. But he played the fish very slowly, as if he were in a

THE DREAM-MAKER
47

trance. "I told him he needed to bear down on the fish because there are only two things that could happen: he would land the fish or he would lose it," says Huff. "Little did I know there was actually a third scenario."

With the fish still on his line, Watkins suddenly collapsed face-first onto the bow. Huff broke off the fish and ran back to the dock at full speed. "He was blue when they loaded him onto the ambulance," Huff says. It turned out that Watkins had an aortic aneurysm and was dead before he hit the deck. "I felt really bad and I asked his buddy what we should do," Huff says. "He told me Everett would have wanted us to go back and fish. So we did. And we caught two nice tarpon." The incident spawned more than a few bad jokes. "People said, 'Damn, Steve, folks really are dying to fish with you,' and 'Why did you break the fish off?'" Huff says.

Luckily, I feel pretty good on this overcast and cool morning as Huff and I make a thirty-minute run into the heart of what Peter Matthiessen called "shadow country"—the vast sky, knotty mangroves, and moving water that are the Everglades.

Huff cuts the engine and hops up on his poling platform. He's wearing a khaki-colored shirt and pants and a pair of closed-toed Crocs. He propels the boat forward with seemingly little effort with his twenty-one-foot pole. We're after snook, the fish that has remained Huff's favorite since his childhood days in Miami.

I stand in the bow and cast a yellow streamer that Huff devised. ("It doesn't have a name. It's just deer hair and chicken feathers," he says.) The wind from an incoming storm is brisk but not unbearable. I'm not exactly throwing strikes with every cast. I start to press a bit, and the casts get even worse. Huff gives me an essential pointer: "Just hold your back cast a bit longer," he says. I quickly see positive results. Huff poles us along, fifty feet or so from the bank. Almost immediately, I start getting solid takes, and within an hour I've landed five smallish (two- to four-pound) snook.

I ask Huff if he thinks different fish have different personalities. "They sure do," he replies. Tarpon, he says, seem almost human because they're so big. "You can see their actual gestures and can tell if they are happy or agitated. I've actually seen them yawn and stretch. It's hilarious." Fishing for them, he adds, "is like heroin."

Bonefish are the most honest fish. "If you do everything right—cast and manipulate the fly—they will reward you and eat it," Huff says. Permit, on the other hand, are dishonest. "You can do everything exactly right and they will still screw you," he says. Snook "are pickpockets. They are sinister. They're always around, but you rarely see them. Then they sneak up on you and strike the fly so savagely."

Huff has made a case study on the nature of anglers, too. He's seen men who can cast a country mile and land the fly on a dime but who couldn't catch a fish in an aquarium. He's seen others who have ugly casts and manage to catch everything they see. "Some people just have a fish sense," Huff says. "I don't care what someone's cast looks like. I'd rather have a person who has some sense of where the fly should be and how to manipulate it and talk the fish to the fly." I'm hoping that with the imperfect casts I'm tossing, I fall into the latter category.

Huff and I talk about our families (he has three grown children) and relationships (Patty, to whom he's been married for twenty-six years, is his second wife; they met through her father, who was a client of Huff's). Huff is a voracious reader and likes to discuss books. But as he talks, I notice that he's constantly eyeing the water in front of us and beyond, looking for any signs of fish. I follow his lead and shift into deep concentration between conversations.

Huff sees a dark mangrove stump in the water near the shore. "Cast right around that," he says. "I think I see something." I cast, make two strips, then my fly is brutally attacked. Water sprays three feet into the air. It's a snook. As it heads for the mangroves, Huff calmly tells me to tighten up on him a bit. After another strong run, I get the snook near the boat and start to bend down in preparation for landing it. "Just wait," Huff says. "He's got one more good run in him." Sure enough, the snook takes off, burning line through my fingers.

THE DREAM-MAKER

When I finally get him to the boat, he weighs in at eight pounds, my biggest snook ever.

We motor to another shoreline. Just as Huff starts poling, he points to a spot a few feet from the bank. "See that shadow?" he asks. "That's a good one." I miss the intended spot (a few feet from the fish's nose) by a good margin. The fish responds anyway, slowly stalking the fly. "That's a fifteen-pounder," Huff whispers. I try to tease the fish with the fly, but I'm running out of room. Five feet away, the fish shoots off, spooked. Only later will I learn what a true trophy a fifteen-pound snook is on a fly.

After a half-dozen more snook, we head in. The wind has picked up, whitecapping the water. Huff would normally stay out, but I have to catch a plane. I feel honored to have shared a day with Huff. He makes me feel like the honor was all his.

Guiding is an incredibly taxing vocation on both mind and body, especially for saltwater flats guides, who may push a boat manually with a pole for up to ten hours a day. Most guides, like NFL running backs, last three to four years. In his younger days, Huff once went five straight months on the water without a break. The physical toll of his guiding is visible only on his hands. His fingernails are gnarled and scratched white. His puffy palms are covered with nicks and cuts. The backs of his hands are speckled with liver spots.

Huff still maintains the pace of men a third his age. But by his own standards, he has slowed down, if only a bit. Now he takes weekends off to spend more time with Patty, who is the editor and publisher of the Everglades City paper, *The Mullet Rapper*. But he is rarely idle. He doesn't own a computer. ("It's appalling to me that people spend a beautiful day indoors staring at a glass screen," he says.) He runs nine miles every Saturday. He's become an avid bicyclist. A few years back, he and Patty rode their bikes from their house in Florida to Astoria, Oregon. Then they rode back.

But even with the biking and running, Huff can't spend more than a few days away from the water. His passion is bringing people into his world of mangroves and tides and fish and the fulfillment of dreams.

"I love what I do," he says.

2011

9

Bone Home Me

On this half-mile-long flat, just around the corner from our rented cottage, dozens of fish are tailing, turning a dark belt of turtlegrass—aurally, at least—into a trout pool in the throes of a heavy mayfly hatch. I pick one fish and stalk it, slowly. It's a tailer that resembles Lawrence more than James, if you get my drift. I make a cast, my first to a fish on this midwinter sojourn to a Bahamian island.

The cast is horrid. I nearly plonk the bonefish on its head. The fish flushes noisily. Then the entire flat goes haywire. Acres of previously unseen fish—many more than seem possible—explode away from the scene in every conceivable direction, the Big Bang in miniature. Perhaps the Creator was a clumsy caster, too.

But, as the trip goes on, there is progress. Some casts fall in the right place. Most knots hold. Fish are held in hand and admired, briefly. Ardent anglers usually right the ship, at least a little, in an attempt to feed the limitless hunger of obsession. Such progress, one hopes, is also found in daily lives—as spouses, parents, and friends, or in jobs.

These fish are big, ocean-goers, black of back. They are spooky as hell. Charlie and I gradually lengthen the leads on our casts, from three feet, to six, even to ten, hoping to somehow divine the fish's route. But even then, on many occasions, as we kneel like religious supplicants and leave our offerings on the bright white sand, a bonefish approaches, heart throttles chest . . . and the fish spazzes out upon sight of a totally inert size 4 Gotcha.

There are cruising fish—singles, doubles, and trebles—zigzagging the sand flats, picking up food where available, like dinner-deprived guests at a cocktail party hunting down the hors d'oeuvre plate handlers.

There are schools that seem to come out of nowhere, startling in their squadron-like formations.

There are mudding fish, appearing as black as tadpoles in the plumes of pale brown.

But it always seems to come back to those tailers near the cottage, those home fish that, though often surrounded by their brethren, are each, individually, wholly consumed in solitary pursuit. Not unlike a bonefishermen on a trip with a good friend.

Oh, and there are permit, too. Only a few, but enough to get the gears in the head turning over all the possibilities. One day, Charlie has a decent shot at a twenty-pounder, its head down, its tail up. But the permit, as a fish, carries with it some baggage for the angler, who is weighed down by the aura, the difficulty, the cult-like status, and even the cult itself, which has among its membership a few who, like some European soccer fans, seem to enjoy the fandom more than the actual sport.

Charlie's hand becomes inexplicably heavy, and he splashes a short cast. The permit speeds away without even a glance at the fly, searing itself into memory.

And there is calamity. There always is in a self-guided week in foreign waters. The dinghy we rely on to get to the surrounding flats never feels exactly seaworthy, tippy in its V-shaped aluminum hull. The old Evinrude, with its pull cord, is even more discomfiting, fussy as a three-month-old baby. On our last day, on an island that's two desolate miles from the home mooring, it finally gives up the ghost. Perhaps we'd run it aground one time too many?

Eventually, a conch fisherman trills by, unhurried. We flag him down. He immediately tells us—in that mellifluous white Bahamian accent, with its hints of the Queen's English—that his motor had flaked on him just the day before, and he'd been forced to return to harbor in reverse.

His face is parched by decades in the sun. His story immediately puts its two mechanically challenged listeners at ease. We are no longer helpless Yankee tourists, but instead compatriots in the ongoing battle against balky boat motors. He jury-rigs the Evinrude so we can make it back home, grinding across the channel at a bovinely pace.

We make it to our flat half an hour before sunset. We have just enough time to look for tails.

2012

10

X Marks the Spot

About fifteen years ago, my uncle introduced me to a spot in the Bahamas. Entrusted me, really, as if it were some priceless family heirloom, to be handled with care.

The spot has about all one could ask for. It's not too far away from "civilization"—a gas station, a small grocery store, and a liquor store that carries pretty much only the essentials (rum, Bahamian beer, ice). The house is nothing fancy, but it has comfortable beds and a decently outfitted kitchen. It sleeps three, max, which is a good number for a do-it-yourself bonefishing trip, and one or two shy of the number of hardcore anglers who really know about the place, at least that I'm aware of. It comes with a ten-foot dinghy, powered by a fifteen horsepower Evinrude motor that is mostly reliable, but just coughy enough to keep you focused. The house is surrounded by flats—some you can walk to, others require boat transport—with enough of a variety of white sand and tailing turtlegrass that you can usually work out a good full day's wading schedule, regardless of the tides. The bonefish are big and fussy. I've seen one school of permit there.

I've long referred to the spot as "the Point," as a way of sort of forcing myself to keep a lid on its existence and whereabouts. I've never once in my life—even when I was younger and even stupider than I am now—been tempted to write a story about it.

The Point has a handful of low-slung houses, mostly owned by conchs and a few Americans who dropped out back in the 1960s. They're old folks now who have been there for a long time, through multiple hurricanes, economic booms and busts, and a pandemic. A few of them rent out their places, but not too many. The Point is quiet. When I go in midwinter, there are rarely any other fishermen around.

Anyway, I was down there this winter with my two friends. We had it all during the five days we were there—a few snotty weather days, some bluebird calm ones (which were the toughest fishing-wise), some very nice, hard-earned fish, a scare when the boat motor wouldn't start while we were on a flat a long swim from home. I have the remnants of a spectacular raccoon-eye sunglasses tan. I still have a scab from the line-burn on my forefinger that conjures memories of specific fish.

We had a blast, as always. Until one night, when we met a man.

Most of us who have dedicated ourselves to this sport have had, at one time or another, a spot we would consider secret. Finding these spots is never easy: it requires time on the water, intuition, and work, and a willingness to leave the crowds and well-known areas and explore—all of which can mean fishless days or weeks. The spots can be well off the beaten path and difficult to get to. They can also be hidden in plain sight. Yes, there are serendipitous discoveries of secret places. But that good luck is usually earned.

Secret spots fall into a strange gray area. There are not "yours," even if you found them. You're not Ponce de León claiming Florida for Spain, my man. And yet, they sometimes *feel* like they're yours, like there should be some unwritten rule that's upheld in this instance. In the Yeti-produced film *120 Days*, the Panhandle tarpon guide, David Mangum, gave his take on discovered spots.

"Nobody owns the ocean," he said. "But you own the intellectual capital that you earned with your blood and sweat over the years."

I'm not sure I agree with Mangum. But I'm not sure I disagree with him, either.

I have some secret spots near my home, places that, in a not insignificant way, are the reason I still live where I do. I guard them fiercely. When I've seen other fly anglers approach, I've scurried into the dunes or broken off hooked fish. I've also just sat down by the water and tried to look as clueless as possible.

"Anything going on here?"

"Nah, haven't seen a thing."

I once had a secret spot on a well-known Atlantic salmon river in Nova Scotia. It was on a bend of river between two named and well-known pools, fat water that had no real areas for salmon to stop and hold . . . except for one, which I discovered when I took my kids tubing on a hot afternoon. As I floated through the middle of the river, I saw that there was, in five feet or so of water by the bank, a huge log that had created a concavity on the river bottom. And in that concavity, I glimpsed four bars of silver, stacked up and finning. A pause lie.

Early the next morning, I returned with my fly rod and caught a salmon. I had the spot to myself for years. I would fish it every summer when I was there with my family. I would fish it again in the fall when I returned to fish with my uncle. It produced with as much regularity as you could ask for when it comes to Atlantics. It was my little secret, and I began to think it would be an everlasting one at that.

But there's one thing that's almost always true about these spots: they rarely remain secrets forever. One morning in the summer of 2018, I trudged out to my spot. Wisps of mist rose from the water. I had grown perhaps a bit careless. I didn't notice the two anglers who were a football field upriver from me until it was too late. I hooked two fish that day from my spot. As I fought the second fish, I finally noticed the duo. They were not casting, but standing in the middle of the river, staring at me. I seized up. I yelled, weakly and without any real conviction, "they're just trout!" hoping they would buy the rather lame lie.

They didn't. The next morning, as I walked upriver to my spot, they were both there, casting to my log, in full concentration, never noticing my presence. It has since become a rather popular spot, to the point that I rarely check it out anymore. Doing so only brings back the pain.

In 2021, I interviewed Casey Sheehan, the CEO of Simms, about fly-fishing's incredible pandemic boom. We talked a bit about crowding on rivers and, remembering my old Nova Scotia pause lie, I asked him what one should do if a favorite secret spot is suddenly overrun. "Go find another one," he said. Sensible advice, of course, and this is what I have done on my Nova Scotia river, though I have yet to find a spot quite as productive as my first.

But that advice does little to console. It's hard to describe the utter despondency that accompanies the loss of a secret fishing spot. It feels like the Fall of Man, a stripping away of some sort of innocence—unfair, but also a revealing of your naked covetousness.

On our last night in the Bahamas, we decided to get dinner at a watering hole about twenty minutes away—beers, fried food, classic rock, an old Herschel Walker USFL jersey hanging on the wall, mostly locals. We were feeling good, satiated, with just a touch of the subdued melancholy that hits when it's time to leave and reenter the real world.

There was a guy there, hanging out at the bar by himself. He saw that we were Americans, and came over and sat with us. We'll call him X. X was one of those people, it was clear right away, who talks incessantly, only pausing to draw breaths when you murmur an "um-hmm." His head was a gleaming cue ball. He wore a pea-green sweatsuit that was baggy, but not in a cool way, if that makes any sense. On his chest, he had two big gold chains on which hung two big gold medallions. It was tough to tell which look he was gunning for: 2010s Mac Miller? Or 2020s Crypto Bro? Maybe both. He told us he was a developer from the mid-Atlantic.

In any event, at some point within his dysenteric verbal barrage, he told us he owned some property on the Point.

"What?" I said, finally getting in an actual word.

Yes, the Point. He had bought the house that was known locally as the Vessel, an old dark home that indeed looked a bit like a ship. The yard around it was always what stood out the most—it was scattered with old buoys, lobster traps, and other ocean ephemera, and various gnomes and yard tchotchkes. When we first arrived at the Point for our trip, I had noticed the Vessel was gone, but I couldn't tell what was taking its place. I would stop by the next day to peek around the fence and see three large light blue buildings. The beginning. "All of those old people on the Point are getting older and dying," X said. "I'm going to buy up their places, too."

He laid out his grand plan enthusiastically, as if we were onboard with it, in his corner. He was building a grand lodge, he said, the "biggest and baddest one in the Bahamas," for bonefish, offshore fishing (his favorite), and dove and boar hunting. He was going to have a fleet of skiffs to work the local flats and a few Hatteras boats. He named a few high-profile sporting lodges in the Bahamas. "We're going to knock the shit out of them."

I sat, stunned into silence, exchanging quick glances with my buddies. Here we were, face-to-face with the guy who was going to destroy something we dearly loved. I didn't know whether to cry into my beer or throw it in his face. I did neither. Would it have mattered?

We left the bar shortly thereafter, speaking very little in the car, then left for home the next morning. As we passed the old Vessel property, we saw workers in the driveway.

I had to remind myself this is the way it is. Biscayne Bay was once an untrammeled angling paradise. McGuane, Harrison, Valdène, and Chatham had the flats around Key West basically to themselves for years. The Marquesas were once someone's spot. You used to be able to easily get a parking spot at the Nature Conservancy water on Silver Creek. The modern world, with its wide open maw of consumerism and connectivity, is swift and heartless. Development is inevitable and unrelenting. The most persistent rule in life is that nothing remains the same.

But I also had to remind myself that this never really "my" spot to begin with, and I "owned" nothing there, intellectual or otherwise. It was also, of course, a true first-world problem. I was (probably) losing a fishing spot, not a limb, for God's sake. Still, it would haunt me, and it hurt. Maybe like a phantom limb.

It is not in my nature to wish another human ill will (well, most other humans) because I do believe a bit in karma. I will certainly not wish X any ill will, though I am also not rooting for him to succeed. The Bahamas, as we all know, can be a place where big dreams don't always come to fruition.

So, for now, I will hold my breath and occasionally keep an eye on X's "progress" via social media. My friends and I will return next year to see what's up. If it's ruined, so be it. We had a great run. Then I will do the inevitable and move on and start looking for my next last, best place.

2022

11

Difficulty

In the spring, standing in the bow of a skiff in the Everglades, I squint through water made mildly turbid by the peat bogs and the general flush of freshwater and tides, searching for the telltale silvery glow of a laid-up tarpon. On a good two-day trip here, I'll spot, and then cast to, close to fifteen tarpon. Maybe six of those sightings will be consummated with the union of a good-enough cast to a willing fish, who will take the fly and provide that "momentary stay against confusion," as Frost wrote, the complete emptying of the mind that satisfies the true jones in fishing. Maybe three of *those* fish will stay on long enough to be brought to hand and released. And that is enough.

"Men are born for games. Nothing else," says the Judge in Cormac McCarthy's *Blood Meridian*. "Every child knows that play is nobler than work."

Fly-fishing is play, a game, a sport, and if anything makes it noble, it is its difficulty. What we respond to in life—in art, in sport—is the struggle against limitations. This is the reason we use a net in the game of tennis, as McGuane once wrote.

There's a flat I hit in the summer that sometimes pours with stripers. The fish come from the deeper water, up and over a shelf onto the sandy shallows, in singles and doubles and, in rare cases, bigger groups than that. They range from five to twenty pounds. They are extremely skittish, likely due to the very busyness of the area around their little flat, what with the boats, the SUPers, the bait guys, and the occasional waverunner. It does not take much for the fish to bolt from the flat like spooked fawns.

The stripers on this flat do not like Clousers. The clear water exposes fraudulence. A crab pattern, tugged slowly along the bottom, leaving little billows of sand in its wake, is really the only fly that will attract any attention. Even then, the fish remain pissy. Most days—when the shots number in the twenties—I'll get only half-hearted follows and no connections. I fish this flat at least fifteen times a year during the prime months and, in good years, land five or six fish. It is easily some of the most fun fishing I've ever done.

Pursuing difficult fish requires an optimism that sometimes must be forced. It demands patience, problem-solving, and an appreciation for nuance. All these things are like muscles: work them harder and they get stronger.

It is said that there are "stages" fly fishermen go through in their angling lives, from wanting to catch a fish—any fish—to wanting to catch many fish, to wanting to catch the biggest fish. The final stage is the desire to catch difficult fish. By design, that means you will catch fewer fish. That, in the end, may be the point.

In the late summer and early fall, there is the Margaree River in Cape Breton. It's public water and usually fairly crowded. The pools are shared with the utterly competent and incompetent alike, making the fishing days as much about studying Man as they are about studying fish. I cast downstream,

DIFFICULTY 63

follow my swing until the dangle at the end, take a few steps downriver, and then cast again. I do this for most of the available sunlight hours every day for a week. There is a maxim in Atlantic salmon fishing that one fish landed makes for a great day. On the Margaree, it's a bit different. One fish a trip is considered a success. It is one of my favorite places to fish in the world.

There are some who have suggested there may be an even higher stage for fly fishermen, some sort of state of total enlightenment, in which the fishing is done with hookless flies. Though I recognize I am ever-evolving, that's a stage I'll likely never attain. This is still a blood sport, whether we release our fish or not, and we should wrestle with the morality of fishing for sport from time to time. Actually catching a fish is still the ultimate goal. Fishing for difficult fish is mainly about the process. We've been told that this process—really, the journey—is the entire point, in fishing and in life. Surely, this is true. But the process has no meaning without a desired yield. Without a fixed destination, there is no meaningful journey to undertake.

Finally, in the fall, it's back to the salt, to try for false albacore and, maybe, bonito. I choose to fish from the shore. There is a more effective and efficient way to target hardtails—with a boat, you can chase the rampaging fish, which come up and down quickly and erratically, and catch dozens in a day. On the shore, it is a waiting game. The fish need to come into casting range. They do so only sporadically. On some days, they don't do it at all. But with time and persistence and a dash of luck, I will get one. It will take out all of my line and much of my backing. The handle on my whirring reel will rap my knuckles. And it will be among the most satisfying fish of the year.

2019

12

The Passion of Andy Mill

ndy Mill stands on the poling platform in the stern of his Hell's Bay flats boat, scanning the water before him, searching for signs of tarpon. A stiff wind luffs his camouflage fishing pants like a sail and threatens to whitecap the water even in this relatively protected inner basin in the Florida Keys. Ten other tarpon boats are within view, everyone, it seems, seeking the lee. No one has caught a fish yet. A few tarpon are rolling in the distance, but nothing is happening near us. I decide to take advantage of that fact to ask Mill a question.

"Andy, what's the key to being a great tarpon fly angler?"

Without hesitating—or taking his eyes off the water—he answers, "You have to show the fly to the fish without him seeing it."

I look to the bow, where Mill's son Nicky stands—compact and alert—his tarpon rod in his right hand, the fly in the fingers of his left. Nicky just nods in agreement. A few minutes later, with the Zen-like koan still bouncing around in my head, Mill suddenly and emphatically whispers, "Nicky. Off the stern. Five o'clock."

Nicky turns, spots the fish, and throws a backhanded cast. He makes one strip, his line comes tight, and the sea explodes in white froth as the fish makes the first of five miraculous, head-shaking jumps. Nicky fights the tarpon hard from the start, pinching his fly line against the butt of the rod and pulling with his entire body. Mill coaches from the stern. "Turn his head, Nicky. Turn it . . . Good, *good.*"

As the fish nears the boat, Nicky pulls even harder and the fish flips, its tail over its head—the finishing blow. "Great job, buddy!" Mill says. Anglers in the other boats have stopped casting to watch. Moments later, after just a twenty-minute fight, the one-hundred-pound fish is alongside the boat. It's quickly revived and then disappears with a powerful flick of its tail.

"I love you, buddy," Mill says as he embraces his son.

Andy Mill is a former member of the US Ski Team, one of the best American racers of his era. He has covered some of the biggest events in sports as a broadcaster for all the major television networks. He had a high-profile marriage to the tennis player Chris Evert, which ended in an even more high-profile—and painful—divorce.

But to those in a certain smallish but fanatical subset of this vast world, Mill is known primarily as one of the best tarpon fly anglers—if not *the* best—who ever lived. He's won more tarpon tournaments than anyone else. He has come up with game-changing innovations in the sport and improved on the work of others who came before him. He's caught thousands of tarpon. In his best year, he landed 107 in just over fifty days of fishing. A man once paid $10,000 to fish with him (Mill donated the money to an Aspen ski club). Mill's cast, even with the big tarpon rod and a twenty-five-mile-an-hour wind in his face, is graceful and unhurried, exactly how you picture the perfect cast (his girlfriend goes so far as to describe it as "sexy"). He wrote the must-have coffee-table book *A Passion for Tarpon* in 2010. "As a tarpon angler, he's so much better than anyone else that I've seen it's almost unfair," says Dustin Huff, a well-respected tarpon guide in the Keys. "He brought a lot of popularity to the sport, somewhat to my dismay as a guide. He made it look so easy and cool that everyone wanted to try it."

Some of his fishing friends refer to Mill as Peter Pan. They mean it in a positive way. He is exuberant and exceedingly warmhearted and loves

THE PASSION OF ANDY MILL

to share his knowledge. At sixty-three, he remains constantly at play (fishing, hunting, golfing, biking, skiing) and in great shape (he hiked a hundred miles bowhunting for elk last fall). His long black hair, streaked with only a few strands of white, sprouts from the top of his head and spills over his fishing visor. A few years ago, he made the AARP magazine's list of "sexiest men over 50." Only the wrinkles near his eyes—from decades spent on water and snow—betray his age.

For the past five years, Mill and Nicky have rented a house in the lower Keys for five weeks during the spring tarpon season. They call it the Poon House. (This name is a bit less prurient than it may seem. In the fly-fishing world, *poon* is shorthand for tarpon.) It functions as some sort of father-son nirvana. The Mills rarely host guests or fish with anyone else while down there. The kitchen table has been requisitioned as a fly-tying station, strewn with hooks and feathers. Tucked in various corners of the house and its garage are bikes, golf clubs, paddleboards, and at least three dozen rods. An opened bag of Fritos rests on a pantry shelf. Good dark rum holds down one corner of the kitchen counter. There's an archery target in the backyard. When the neighbors are out of town, the Mills sneak over to their yard to practice longer shots. They eat dinner on the couch and watch the Golf Channel. Breakfast is usually a bowl of cereal with bananas and a very strong cup of coffee. They go to bed at around nine every night and are usually among the first boats on the water in the morning.

Nicky, who is twenty-two, is the middle of the three sons Mill fathered with Evert. The father and son spend a lot of time together. They bow hunt for elk, golf, ski, and mountain bike. Nicky caught his first tarpon on the fly when he was fourteen. "He is my best friend in the world, and I'm fortunate that he gravitated to the things I love," Mill says. "My other boys haven't, and that's fine, of course."

This season is a special one, though. Nicky, following in his father's large footsteps, has entered two upcoming tarpon tournaments, the youngest angler in both. Mill, who says he's retired from tournament angling, has spent the spring coaching his son. The father has a lot of lessons to offer, about tarpon fishing and, more important, about all the joy and heartbreak and possibilities for redemption that constitute a full life.

Mill was born in Fort Collins, Colorado, and lived for a while in Wyoming. When he was eight, his father, who was in the lumber business, moved the family to Aspen. One year later, Mill got into ski racing and quickly emerged as a prodigy. At sixteen, he made the US Ski Team's development squad. Five years later, in 1974, he jumped to the A team, and for the next seven years he was the best downhiller in the United States.

With that talent came a rebellious streak. "This was post-Vietnam," Mill says. "It was kind of an anarchic time." He was known for taking the riskiest lines on the course during the day, then partying with the Europeans all night. He had a long mane of hair and an unruly beard. He was the first skier to decorate his helmet with art—an eagle clutching an American flag, airbrushed by a motorcycle-racing friend. He clashed a bit with his coaches. Once, when they asked him to cut his hair, he got a perm instead. ("I looked like a white Jimi Hendrix," he says.) His American ski buddies called him Downhill Jesus. The Europeans nicknamed him the *Wilde Hund* (wild dog).

Mill would represent the United States in two Olympics and two World Championships, and win one US Alpine championship. But his promise as a racer went unfulfilled (though he had seven top tens in World Cup events, he never made the podium), marred mostly by injuries. During his career, he broke an arm, his wrist, his neck, his back, and both legs. He had a total of eleven surgeries on his knees, and has had his left one replaced. "Life should not be a journey to the grave with the intention of arriving safely in a pretty and well-preserved body," Mill says, quoting Hunter S. Thompson.

Injuries, though, tell only part of the story. Mill was a world-class talent. He won many training runs in his career. "I just didn't have the composure to win when it counted," he says. "I was a little too emotional, and I didn't know how to contain it. I choked a bit on race days. I could have used a mentor."

The highlight of his racing career came in the downhill in the 1976 Olympics at Innsbruck, Austria. An injury was involved, of course. Mill

THE PASSION OF ANDY MILL

fell during his first training run and sustained a boot-top bruise on his right leg so severe that he needed crutches to get around. On the day of the race, he sat by the starting gate, his bare leg buried deep in the snow for an hour to dull the pain. Despite not being able to feel his leg as he raced, Mill finished sixth, four tenths of a second from a bronze medal. (Twelve years later, he would receive a US Olympic Spirit Award for that run.)

It was in the 1981 season, Mill says, that everything started to come together. Though he was, at twenty-seven, the team's oldest member, he was (relatively) healthy. More important, he says, "I finally felt like I got it. I finally figured myself out." Early in the season, he placed fourth in a downhill in Italy, his best result ever. A month later, at the famous Lauberhorn downhill in Wengen, Switzerland, he was nearing the end of his first training run when he misread the last jump and, at fifty miles an hour, crashed face-first into a frozen fence. Somehow, he managed to walk to the helicopter that airlifted him to a clinic in town. "I was thinking about how I could get the kink out of my neck so I could race the next day."

By the time Mill landed in Wengen, he told the medics to put him on a backboard and take him to a proper hospital. "Something felt really wrong," he says. It turned out he had broken his neck and back, and torn all the ligaments in his right knee. His skiing career was over. "I just ran out of body," he says.

Mill went back to Aspen with no job and no money. He came up with an idea for a five-minute TV show, called *Ski with Andy Mill*, aimed at ski resorts, offering tips for both beginners (how to walk in ski boots) and experts (how to ski in trees). Soon his show was airing at eighty-two resorts across the country.

That led to opportunities. Mill became a special correspondent for *Good Morning America*. He did some work for ESPN and NBC. He was a commentator for CBS during the 1992 and 1994 Winter Olympics. Later he hosted a fishing show called *Sportsman's Journal* on the Outdoor Life Network for seven years. In all, Mill carved out a twenty-year career in broadcasting. The TV work was fine, he says, but he felt unsatisfied, missing the rush competitive skiing had once provided. He would find that again in another sport.

⊶

Mill has roots in fly-fishing as much as he does in skiing. At age nine, he got his first fly-casting lesson. It happened to come from the legendary angler-author Ernest Schwiebert, who was in Aspen for a clinic. By fourteen, Mill was guiding and tying flies for the local shop. He fished for trout every summer. He took along a fly rod when training in Europe and South America with the US Ski Team.

While on a trip to Belize thirty years ago, Mill hooked his first two tarpon. Though he failed to land either, "I thought, 'This is the most insane thing I've ever seen.' It was like a bolt of lightning had struck me and I had survived." Having now caught permit, bonefish, steelhead, Atlantic salmon, giant trevallies, and marlin on a fly, he says, "The tarpon bite is the greatest in fishing. If anyone says otherwise, they've never had one." In tarpon fishing, he'd found something that provided some of the same feelings that racing had—anxiety, adrenaline, chaos, solitude—without, for the most part, the threat of severe injury.

For the next seven years, Mill fished for tarpon for at least forty days a year, mainly with the guide Harry Spear. Then he set his sights on the Keys tarpon tournaments, which had been won in previous years by such legendary fly anglers as Billy Pate and Ted Williams. "Fishing tournaments are kind of an oxymoron," Mill says. "Generally, you fish to get away from pressure and stress. But for me, the tournaments became a way of measuring how good I could be. They gave me a second chance to prove that I could be great at something." (There is an obvious parallel between Williams and Mill, two former world-class athletes who became great tarpon fly fishermen. Williams was better at his given sport, indeed one of the best baseball players of all time; Mill turned out to be the better tarpon angler.)

Mill began entering tarpon tournaments in the late 1990s. He lost an early one by a mere eight ounces after dropping a 125-pound fish at

THE PASSION OF ANDY MILL   71

the boat. But by the turn of the century, he started winning, learning to tame the emotions he couldn't as a ski racer. Beginning in 2000, Mill won five of six Gold Cups, the most prestigious tarpon tournament in the world. (By then, he was fishing with the guide Tim Hoover, after Spear retired.) "I didn't sleep for ten years when I started tournament fishing," Mill says. "I was just obsessed." Tarpon tourneys certainly didn't provide the worldwide fame and remuneration of skiing. Mill didn't care. "I felt vibrant and alive," he says. "I think that anything that keeps you awake for, not nights, but years is worth it."

Mill distinguished himself, says Dustin Huff, with his ability "to catch the fish that didn't want to be caught." There happened to be more of those types of tarpon by the time Mill was fishing tournaments. Tarpon angling had grown in popularity in the 1990s. As a result, the fish—with more pressure—became warier, particularly on the ocean side of the Keys, where migrating schools were forced to navigate a flotilla of boats.

Mill was the first tarpon angler to start using much smaller flies (1/O hooks) and fish with longer leaders, up to fifteen feet. He helped design Hardy's tarpon rods, which are considered among the best in class, lightweight and nearly impossible to break. He used an extra-large arbor reel to more quickly retrieve line. He did unorthodox things while retrieving the fly, like wiggling the tip of his rod to impart movement on the fly. He became obsessed with testing the limits of the tippets he used in tournaments. He first tied his fly line to the bumper of a car and pulled, but that didn't satisfy him. He then bought a Chatillon force gauge to test the tippet, but that required the help of another person. Finally, he settled on a pulley system, with the line attached to a twelve-pound dumbbell. He would lift the dumbbell with his fly rod for hours in his garage, getting his body and mind attuned to exactly how hard you can strike a fish, and how hard you can pull on it during a fight (the answer to both: harder than you think).

He worked equally hard on the water. Most anglers, when faced with an oncoming school of tarpon, will reflexively cast for the lead fish, or just flock shoot. "Andy reads the school and analyzes the situation in a split second, reading the body language of an individual fish," says Paul

Dixon, a Keys guide. Sometimes, there's just something like a mild flare of the gills, or the particular way a fish is swimming. Sometimes it's the color of the fish's back in the water (fish that appear brown are more likely to bite than those that appear black, according to Mill). Other times, it's just something ineffable, a "feel" that comes from experience or instinct.

In 2006, after an astonishing run and with nothing left to prove, Mill retired from tournament angling. Along with the five Gold Cups, he won the tarpon world's Triple Crown (the Gold Cup, the Golden Fly, and the Don Hawley tournaments). "The tournaments were beginning to drive me a bit crazy," he says. "I'd maybe find some satisfaction on the last day of the tournament when I held the trophy. But then I'd immediately start driving myself crazy again."

It so happens that right around this time, his eighteen-year marriage to Evert was nearing its swift and dramatic end.

⚬━━⚬

It's impossible to talk about Mill without talking about his marriage, mainly because Mill so willingly discusses it.

One night, in a crowded Keys fish house, I ask him about Evert. He gets maybe four words out before his face falls and tears begin streaming from his eyes. "I'm sorry, man," he says. "I cry a lot."

Mill first met Evert at a New Year's Eve party at the Hotel Jerome in Aspen in 1986. She'd been invited by her friend and on-court rival Martina Navratilova. Mill sat next to Evert at dinner. The next morning, they skied together. "I had never been on skis, and I was petrified," Evert says. "Andy told Martina that he would get me down the hill. I ended up skipping the Australian Open and staying there with him." A year and a half later, they married.

Mill traveled with her to tennis matches around the world. He met Pope John Paul II and Margaret Thatcher, and became a sort of Forrest Gump figure in US presidential politics. Mill and Evert were with President George H. W. Bush at Camp David the weekend after Iraq

THE PASSION OF ANDY MILL

73

invaded Kuwait. At six o'clock that Sunday morning, Mill heard a knock at his door. "It was President Bush," he says. "He said, 'Andy, I can't sleep. Want to go shoot some skeet?'"

Mill and Evert were also guests of Bill Clinton's at a White House dinner the day after the Monica Lewinsky scandal broke. Mill spent half an hour talking to Clinton about how he was dealing with the fallout and still carrying on with his presidential duties.

Mill and Evert had three boys—Alex, Nicky, and Colton—in a span of five years. The family split its time between their houses in Boca Raton and Aspen. Mill says they did everything together—hiking, fishing, riding motorcycles. "Those were the best times of my life," he says.

It all came to an abrupt halt. "Look, nobody died, but it was a tragedy," Mill says. "We had a great family, a great dynamic, and great passion. And then, all of a sudden, I woke up one day and she's gone, the kids are gone, the house is gone, and we all just got really disconnected. It's been a rough road in a number of ways."

That Evert left Mill for the golfer Greg Norman complicated matters even more. (The two married in 2008 and have since divorced.) Mill recites a rather masterful quote he gave to the Australian media at the time: "Greg Norman at one time was my best friend, and a year and a half ago, I would have taken a bullet for this guy. But I didn't realize he was the one who was going to pull the trigger."

"I totally understand all of that from his perspective," Evert says. "These things just happen. They even happen to good people."

Mill says he cried for three years and lost thirty pounds. "Therapy and Jack Daniel's didn't help," he says. "I couldn't fish or play golf. I was a mess, but I own it. I realize that I had something to do with it. And then, one day, I woke up and decided I was sick and tired of being sick and tired, and got on with life."

Mill and Evert are now great friends. "I love her. She's the mother of my children. We still have a great family. She asked me the other day if I would be there with her on her deathbed. I will. And she would be there with me on mine." Says Evert: "We have each other's backs, for sure."

Just as Mill is wiping away the tears, a man walks up to our table, as if scripted. "Are you *the* Andy Mill?" he asks. "Do you mind if I get a picture with you?"

"I'd be honored," Mill says, as a smile quickly returns to his face.

⚬━━⚬

Before the 2015 Golden Fly Tournament, Mill received a phone call from Rob Fordyce, a guide. Fordyce's angler had dropped out. He wanted to know if Mill, nearly a decade removed from his last tournament, would fill in. Mill said yes.

Mill and Fordyce began the last day of the tournament close to 180 pounds behind the leader, a seemingly insurmountable deficit. But Mill landed two big fish that day to come from behind and win (his sixth Golden Fly title). "That was the last one," he says. "I swear."

Now, he says, he fishes out of pure enjoyment. "The game played with these fish is so compelling. I've been fascinated with it for three decades now. Every fish is different. Every cast is different."

And, of course, there is Nicky. He is not a carbon copy of his father. His cast is quicker and more powerful but equally effective. Nicky prefers the backhand cast—a useful weapon in the quick-twitch game of tarpon fishing, where fish sometimes appear out of nowhere. That favoritism should come as no surprise given his maternity. Nicky also takes after his mother in his looks and demeanor—the strong cheekbones, the steely squint to his eyes, and the quiet determination that belies fierce competitiveness within.

Mill and Nicky occasionally bicker a bit, as anyone would when spending up to twelve hours a day on a sixteen-foot skiff. ("Dad, you're poling too fast." "No, I'm not." "Yes, you are. Slow down.") But most of the time, the banter is warm and affirmative. ("That was a pretty good cast, right, Dad?" "It was perfect, Nicky.") It reveals two minds that have begun to meld. ("What do you think about pushing off for that bar, Nicky?" "That's exactly what I was thinking.")

THE PASSION OF ANDY MILL

Nicky says he's not sure if he wants to become a full-time tournament angler. But, as his father once did, he believes it's time to see just how good he's become. In the process, it seems, something more important has been found. "I love being out here with him every day and seeing his heart and passion," Mill says. "I'm just really proud of him."

2016

13

Salmon Season

It starts in high summer, in Labrador, that land of windswept crags, quaking bogs, and enthusiastic blackflies. "The land God gave to Cain," as the explorer Cartier described it. Well, it is my sincere hope that the fratricidal sumbitch took along a fly rod.

I sure did. I'm on assignment, chasing down a mineral prospector who hit it big—really big—when he stumbled upon what would eventually become the world's richest nickel mine. He's done various things with his considerable dough. One of them: a lodge on the Hunt River in northern Labrador, just seventy miles or so from the spot of his fortunate discovery. The man is wholly obsessed with fishing. After hearing about his annual angling program—three months in Labrador chasing Atlantic salmon, six months hunting tarpon in the Keys—it's unclear to me how exactly he manages to run his various mining businesses and venture capital funds. The man is from Newfoundland, and he fishes in the willful manner characteristic of folks from his island. He does not like to rotate through pools, preferring instead to find a fish he favors, then casting over it until he or the fish succumbs. He once spent nine straight hours on a single fish, pausing only to sip water. He eventually landed the twenty-five-pound Atlantic.

I meet him in Labrador, a place where there seems to be more black bears than people. It's an ideal spot for introverts with bear spray. One day, the man invites me to join him on the upper Hunt, above the mammoth first falls. The section was never fished by the previous owners of his camp. There are twenty pools on the upper section. Only seven of them are named. The camp rule: if you land and release an Atlantic of twenty or more pounds in an unnamed pool, you get naming rights. The hair stands up on the back of my neck when I'm told this. I realize it sounds petty and self-important and self-aggrandizing, this chance to name your own salmon pool. But it does offer something: a rare shot at a tiny slice of angling immortality. Salmon pools are sacred things and are rarely, if ever, renamed.

The man and I take a bumpy, uncomfortable ride in an ATV on a rough-cut trail that leads to a canoe tied to a tree above the falls. We work our way upstream. I quickly run through the questions I have for the man to get his story. I have fishing on my brain now. The man seems to understand. He cuts to the chase with his answers, giving me what I need. Then we stop at a pool. "This one doesn't have a name yet," he says. I tuck my notebook into my slingpack and tie on a fly, the first of a baker's dozen I will go through that day. I decide to emulate the man. I find two big fish finning in the clear current, two silver logs. One is larger than the other. It's a pool-namer, I am sure of it. The other one?

I start with a dry fly, a big orange-hackled bug, a Labradorian staple. Nothing. I switch to a Blue Charm, a salmon-world staple. Nothing. I pause to take huge slurps of water, to ponder the three-hundred-year-old spruces swaying in the breeze, to listen, when the wind shifts in our direction, to the roar of the falls, and, yes, to run through my list of potential pool names. This feels like a jinx, like I'm thinking too far ahead. But I can't help it. Name it after my wife? That would be the gentlemanly thing to do. Name it after myself? One of my kids? All my kids? After my favorite rock band? My favorite salmon fly?

I keep casting. The day has somehow begun to slip away, the light getting flatter. The man is downstream from me, casting. We are together, but in our own worlds. We have forgotten to eat lunch. I tie on a Green Machine, the fly with which I caught my first Atlantic salmon twenty-three years ago as a teenager. Newfoundlanders fish it like a dry fly. I

SALMON SEASON 79

like to swing it just under the water's surface and watch its wake. I cast. Both fish move, ever so slightly. Blood pounds in my ears. I cast again. The smaller of the two fish lifts off the river bottom and arcs toward the fly and snaps. I set the hook. It's a big fish, big enough that if you lost it, you would say, "It was high teens, maybe twenty."

The man hears the commotion and reels up and makes his way upstream to me, putting on his tailing glove as he wades. I lead the fish to him. He expertly grabs its tail. I hold my breath as I walk down to him. "Nice fish," he says. "Really nice." My throat is parched. I know the answer already, before I even see the fish. The man looks at me and shrugs. I grab ahold of the fish. Its gills pump in oxygen. And then I let my fifteen-pounder go.

⚬══╾⚬

It ends in the early fall, with my last cast on the Margaree River in Cape Breton, Nova Scotia. This is a public river. You do not pound a single fish here. The local unwritten rule: make a cast, retrieve it, step down. I'm on a family vacation. Wife and kids. We are at the cabin, just finished. But there is more work to be done, the endless fine-tuning. There are hikes and picnics and naps. There is not much time for fishing. One hour in three days, to be exact. I wouldn't have had it any other way.

But on the last morning, I cannot fight the jones. The eight-month-old is up early. I'm on duty. I fix her a bottle as I make myself some coffee. I think, briefly, about waking up my wife, and then, just as quickly, rethink it.

Outside, I put on my waders, string up my rod. I strap the baby into the Bjorn on my chest. I look around self-consciously even though we are in the middle of the woods. What I'm doing may not be illegal, but it certainly lacks common sense. I imagine my photo, with my mouth agape—the face of the guilty—going viral on some social media account that outs stupid dads.

We walk down to the river in front of the cabin. I am relieved no one is in the pool. The morning is cool and windless. I start high in the pool and cast and step, cast and step. The baby strapped to my chest kicks her Michelin Man legs and peers down at the moving water. I can feel her downy hair on my chin.

I reach the sweet spot, right by a huge submerged rock, and slow it all down. I tie on an orange Bomber, cast it, and watch it teeter totter in the light ripples as it drifts over the rock. The fly is crushed. The fish thrashes the water and then leaps and lands with a smacking belly flop. The baby coos with delight. It is a bright fish, large for this river. Its heft and energy pulse through the bent rod. My heart and mind are racing. I wonder how I will land this fish without causing all sorts of trouble? With no plan in mind, I get the fish in close enough to see it. The baby goes still, transfixed. The fish answers my question for me, running and then leaping once more and throwing the hook. The baby snaps out of her trance. I snap out of mine, too. I reel up and we head home.

2014

14

A Lifetime of Atlantic Salmon in a Day

The Morning

I am a teenager. I don't know much worth knowing. We're on Nova Scotia's Margaree River, one of the comeliest slashes of water I've ever seen. It's my first Atlantic salmon trip. With me are my uncle, Charles, and our guide, Ed, a bespectacled and bearded expatriate with reckless teeth. The eight-weight is heavy in my hand. The pool is cloaked in remnants of early morning fog. Snag, the pool is called, which is promising. Or maybe not. It could be loaded with fish. Or it could be mined with a century's worth of sunken, fly-snatching deadfall.

There are six people already in the pool. This is public water. They are all throwing casts, down and across. It is, as I will come to learn over the ensuing years, the most effective way to catch Atlantic salmon. It is also the method that was used by the very first fly fishermen. Atlantic salmon fishing is the Q Document to fly-fishing's many subsequent Gospels.

Charles motions to Ed with a nod. I am to enter the water first, at the top of this congenial conga line that moves downstream in a rhythm unspoken. I have on a Green Machine, a small neon-bright bug with bristles of brown hackle. "Cast now," Ed says through his crooked smile.

I do. It's a disaster, a pileup, a plate of cooked spaghetti spilled onto the river's surface. I look around, self-conscious. No one has noticed. I cast again. This one is better, and the river pulls the line taut. Another cast. This time the line stops, then begins to slice through the water with a distinct *whir*. "Let her run," says Ed. A salmon, the size and color of the Stanley Cup, leaps. I stop breathing. This is how love begins. Ed tails the henfish, then lets her go. Word gets out that it's my first. One by one, the other men in the pool reel up and come and shake my hand, then turn and reassume their spots and start casting again.

The Afternoon

The lunch is, shall we say, boozy. I am in my mid-twenties, sent to this river deep in the wildlands of northern Canada to profile the young heir to a massive global fortune. The young heir owns part of this river, along with the handsome house positioned at the river's mouth, where it empties into the Gulf of Saint Lawrence. It's his show here. We all follow his lead. When he pours a second, third, fourth glass of wine at lunch, we drink them. This is decidedly not the salmon fishing I read about in Schwiebert and Knight. This is rock and roll. We're out of bed early despite the headache. We fish hard in the morning until lunch when the wine is poured like a liquid offering to the gods. Then we fish again in an afternoon haze, with the sole aim of keeping a hook out of the back of our heads. We limit out every day.

One night, we sit outside around a bonfire on the beach, staring into it, atavistically transfixed. Libations and conversations flow. Eventually, I start to feel a bit woozy. It has been a long week, and it has to be well after midnight, so I decide it's time to go to bed. I stand to say good night and the earth suddenly lurches off its axis. I stumble toward the fire but right myself just in time to avoid it, landing facedown in white sand as soft as powdered sugar. I am mortified. I am here, supposedly, as a professional, to write a story. I start to stand, brushing off the sand, composing an apology in my head for my appalling behavior, when I turn around and see the young heir and our other two companions face-first in the sand as well. After a brief moment of silent recognition, we all begin to cackle into the dark night.

When I get back to the cabin, I check my watch. It's eight-thirty P.M.

The Evening

Joe, my guide, inhales the white smoke of his cigarette. A lungful is exhaled, the smoke now a pale blue. He lifts his fist to his mouth and expels a yellow cough. Joe's like a rainbow.

I'm on the Miramichi on a perfect pool, where two braids of water have come together to form a perfect V, mimicking the patterns formed by the traveling geese high above us. I am in my early thirties, nearly two decades into the sport. It is the end of the season, those late last licks that always get me, that slight melancholy of another mile marker passing right before my eyes. It is cold. The slate gray water hurries by, headed for the Baie des Chaleurs, which is already whipped into the fury of the oncoming incommodious winter. Only a few leaves remain attached to the riverbank trees. In the breeze, these stragglers metronomically twist back and forth, like the wave of the queen's hand. The fish are here, but they are unimpressed by my offerings.

I turn to Joe, seeking the confidence the best guides routinely instill. Joe leans back on a log and expels another thoughtful plume. He tells me to put on an orange bug. A dry fly. It makes no sense at all. The water is too cold. But Joe is a man who believes that when all else fails, go with the least expected move. He might have made for a clever swordsman. I tie on the fly and cast. A nose emerges from the gray and nudges the fly, then inhales it. A grilse. I land two more in the next twenty minutes, all on the dry fly. Then the river—and the season—shuts off, in the gloaming of the late fall.

2012

15

Blind Casting

It was July, and we were on the Pinware River in southern Labrador. I was fishing with the best salmon anglers I know—Billy Taylor, president of the Atlantic Salmon Federation; David Clark, the indefatigable Nova Scotian; and Yvon Chouinard, the all-world fisherman. We were having a tough morning. The weather was miserable—a cold rain blew into our faces from the angry ocean just a mile away. And we were fishless. But the salmon were there—silver half moons leaped all around us.

Shortly after lunch, a young man appeared from the piney woods, leading another man, this one older, silver-haired, by the elbow. They walked to the water's edge and wedged their way between Taylor and Chouinard. The young man stood by the older man's non-casting side and gave him instructions on where to cast. "Two o'clock," or "little longer," that sort of thing.

After maybe five casts, the older man's rod bent into an arc. Salmon. He let the fish run, then reeled hard when it stopped. The salmon leaped, the young man yelled, "Drop the tip!" and the silver-haired man did exactly that. The silver-haired man brought the salmon to his feet, but never looked down. The young man expertly tailed it with his bare hands, then pulled it out of the water. He grabbed the silver-haired man's hand and led it to the fish. The silver-haired man rubbed his two fingers across the salmon's glistening back. Then the young man released it.

The young man repositioned the older one in the water, turning his body so he again faced quartered downstream. A few casts later, he hooked another salmon. Same scene: young man guiding the older man's hand to feel the fish's back, then releasing it.

With that, the young man again held the older man's elbow and led him out of the river. They disappeared into the green pines with the mist.

Once they were gone, I glanced furtively at my companions. Taylor and Clark were bent slightly at the waist, intently minding the swing of their flies through the riffly pool. Chouinard was standing on a red rock mid-river, cracking long casts over the water with his double-handed fly rod. I started casting again. We fished like this, hard and without a word or eye contact, for three more hours. We did not hook a single salmon.

Back at the lodge, we staggered around, silent and exhausted. We picked at the food set in front of us.

After dinner, we lingered at the table. Everyone remained quiet for a while, then Chouinard made a little noise in his throat. We all looked at him. He was leaning his chair back against the wall. He was staring at the bottle of Labatt's Blue in his hand, working on pulling off the label, turning up the corners.

"I tried everything today," he started, addressing his words to the bottle. "Wets, dries, riffle hitch. Dead-drifting the fly. Stripping it. Everything."

We all nodded. *Yes. Yes.*

"I can't believe it," he continued. "I can't believe I was outfished by a blind guy."

He began to chuckle, giddy with exhaustion, and the next thing you knew, it caught on and we all doubled over in laughter. We had suffered the same fate.

When the laughter died down, Chouinard stopped worrying the corners of his beer label. Then he rubbed his head thoughtfully.

"I even tried casting with my eyes closed."

Beer shot through my nose.

2005

16

Power Play

Sitting on a rock by the Rynda River on Russia's Kola Peninsula, the tall man with tousled gray hair and big blue eyes greedily feasts on a piece of rare Moscow beef, the juice running down his fingers. He has spent the morning making graceful casts with his double-handed fly rod. His private MI-2 helicopter, a relic of the Soviet era, is perched on a ridge behind him, the pilot ready to whisk him off to the next salmon pool after lunch. Two quiet Russian fishing guides are hunched over a campfire, cooking him potatoes.

"You know," says the man with a smile. "It's good to be at the top."

In Stockholm, James Prosek, the artist and author, and I board the chartered Embraer 145 jet bound for Murmansk with fifty or so others who hail from Great Britain, Ireland, Scotland, and Sweden. We are the handpicked guests of one Peter C. Power, the sixty-four-year-old millionaire former British industrialist who, for all intents and purposes, owns two camps within two million acres of austere Russian tundra that happens to be veined with four rivers—the Kharlovka, Rynda, Eastern Litza, and Zolotaya—which host some of the last pristine runs of Atlantic salmon in the world.

88   RIVERS ALWAYS REACH THE SEA

On the plane—his charter—there is chatter all around about Peter, who seems to grow more mythical, more mysterious, with each foot of elevation gained over the Finnish Laplands.

"It's like he's the lord of his own fiefdom," an Irishman in the seat behind me says, his eyes incredulously wide. "It truly is." It's his third trip to Peter's camp on the Kharlovka.

"I heard he knows Putin personally, that he can call him anytime he likes," I overhear a Brit in front of me tell his seatmate between sips of gin and tonic.

There are other rumors, of Russian women and big, silvery salmon.

On the plane, James and I sit on either side of Håkan Stenlund, the photographer from Sweden. James insists on calling him "Swenson," for no other obvious reason than liking the sound of it. Swenson has been to Power's camps a dozen times. "Peter is a nice guy," he tells us. "You will like him."

What about the rumors? "Well, you'll find out for yourselves," Swenson says, with an inscrutable grin.

At the airport in Murmansk, the gateway to the Kola, a homely old woman serves us steins of beer as we wait for the helicopters that will take us to the camps. The bar is dank and dirty. The speakers in the ceiling pipe in songs by the J. Geils Band and Foreigner. Our three beers cost $3. I give the old woman a $1 tip. She smiles, flashing a twinkling rack of gold teeth.

We hop into the massive transport helicopter, built during the Cold War. We are each given headphones and told to relax and make ourselves comfortable. The helicopter gasps and lurches as it takes off. Its rattle is felt in our teeth. Some wiring on the ceiling is held together by silver

POWER PLAY 89

duct tape. We gaze out the small windows. Below us, miles and miles of rushing tundra.

When we arrive at the Kharlovka camp we are greeted by Peter. He strides up the wooden walkway to the landing platform accompanied by two stout Russian men and a stunning, petite, blue-eyed, raven-haired young woman. They all walk a half step behind him. We gather around Peter in a semicircle, holding our bags.

"Camp rule number one is that all guests must play hard and work hard," Peter says, smiling. Then his smile drops. "Camp rule number two is that all the women here belong to me."

There are murmurs, half-laughs, among the gathered. They are cut short when they are not reciprocated by Peter.

We walk to our cabins.

I turn to Swenson. Before I can say anything, he tells me, "That's Peter's summer girl."

Despite the fact that I am here to write a story about Peter, I won't lay eyes on him again until four days later.

We fish for three straight days on the Litza, Kharlovka, and Zolotaya. We catch more Atlantic salmon than most salmon anglers will catch in a season. They take swinging wets, dries on top. Most are in the fifteen-to-twenty-pound range. It is feverish.

I am burdened a bit by worry. Every day, I ask when I might be able to speak with Peter. I need to justify the fact that a magazine has sent me here for ten days. "Tomorrow," I'm told, on three successive days. Peter seems to be avoiding me and has gradually grown into some Kurtz-like figure.

Then he shows.

At breakfast, a great black bird of a helicopter swoops down from the sky and lands at the camp. "He's here," someone says.

As the blades *chop-chop-chop* overhead, Peter steps out of the helicopter. He's wearing his waders and cupping a cigarette. He is accompanied by two guides—again a half step behind him—but no woman.

The Russian employees all walk to greet him, hesitant but insistent, a mixture of love and fear in their wary postures. Peter puts them at ease, says hello, shakes their hands. With his left hand, he sweeps the gray hair away from his big blue eyes. In his right hand, he holds his cigarette.

James, Swenson, and I jump into the helicopter with Peter, who sits shotgun, and points to various things with his cigarette as we fly over the camp. There is a homemade ashtray on the helicopter door. We stop first at his new dacha, one that he's building on the Kharlovka to complement the one he already has on the Rynda, up the hill from that camp. "Some people collect art," he tells me. "I collect houses on salmon rivers . . . and art."

We fish that morning for native brown trout on the upper Rynda. The trout are absolutely beautiful, with big black spots on their flanks. They fascinate James.

At lunch, Peter turns to James.

"How do you prefer to be addressed, as James or Jim?"

James says it doesn't really matter, but "James" would be fine.

"Okay, Jim," says Peter.

That night, we move to the Rynda camp and join the festive in-progress "young persons week." Peter's son and his friends are taking Camp Rule Number One to heart. We eat fresh king crabs and drink vodka. Rupert,

POWER PLAY   91

Angus, Duncan, and the rest welcome us into the fold, telling stories about their public school days. Someone produces a guitar after dinner. We sing Don McLean's "American Pie" a half-dozen times. Perhaps the Brits are just being polite.

I fish with Peter for the rest of my time there. He tells me of growing up in the Midlands, of how he—one of six children—rescued the family business after his father died by, essentially, inventing the plastic wrapping that bundles newspapers. It's one of those gee-whiz inventions, like the Post-it Note or Velcro, a little thing perhaps, but one that satisfied a need, then became an absolute necessity. He tells me about selling the company for tens of millions to a US concern, and then, directionless, going on a three-year bender that landed him in rehab. He tells me about emerging from rehab, sober and with a sense of purpose, and how he leased this property—off-limits during the Cold War because of its military bases—for forty-nine years, with the idea of running camps that cost $10,000 a week to fish, then plowing that money into ensuring the health of these last great runs of the threatened Atlantic salmon. He tells me how the Russians viewed him as "an extremely rich nutcase," and how he has his rivers patrolled by guards with Kalashnikovs to discourage poachers, and how he hired bodyguards after receiving death threats. "This is the story of a man who took a while to figure out how to live a great life, then decided he would do so by creating happiness," he says. "It's just magic. Bloody magic."

The rumors about Peter, I decide, all contain within them kernels of truth. Yes, there are summer girls, and yes, Peter has, like Kurtz, gone a bit native. But I figure out that the more prurient rumors mostly originate in the Kharlovka camp, where the guests only see Peter once or twice during their week and have the rest of the time to fill in the blanks with their own versions of his life, like the partygoers at Gatsby's mansion.

Peter becomes, in some odd way, a sympathetic figure, even when he reprimands James and me for not being "serious" salmon fisherman because we do not use double-handed rods.

On our last night in Russia, Swenson and I decide to fish after dinner in the haunting gray gloaming of the late Arctic summer. James stays behind in camp to play guitar. Swenson and I hike a few miles upstream, then hopscotch our way down, fishing each pool with intensity. At midnight, I stop at Peter's Pocket, a small pool boxed in a canyon like a present from the salmon gods, and take a short cast. I think I am hooked on the bottom, and I throw repeated overhand casts to try to dislodge the fly. But the rock suddenly starts moving and I hold on for dear life. For ten minutes, the contest is an even draw, with neither the fish nor me budging. I can tell that it is the biggest salmon I've ever hooked into, possibly over the thirty-pound mark that demarcates a "serious" fish. I want to catch it, for myself and to prove something to Peter. I yell in vain for Swenson, who is nowhere to be seen.

After a while, the fish makes its move. It starts slowly upstream, my line following the beast, then accelerates like no fish I've ever hooked toward the rapids above the pool. It leaps, suspended for a moment in the air, shakes its head and lands, and then surges again. My single-handed rod breaks in half and the fish goes free. I sit on a mid-stream rock, my head in my hands, dazed and exhausted.

2003

17

End of the Season

I.

That night, back in camp, the eight of us—shoulder-sore and wind-burned and half in the bag from the glasses of whiskey—sink into the chairs in the common room of this New Brunswick lodge, indulging in our rite of autumn. The lodge is perched on a bluff overlooking a Miramichi pool, now silent and mysterious, that's a popular gathering place for those prodigal wanderers of the Atlantic Ocean on their long journeys home. There is a whispery rumble in the room, some casual, unfocused one-on-one conversations, but these seem to be warm-ups to some central act. We're waiting for someone to take the ball and run, to step up and entertain.

Someone does. A monologue starts as a low thrum. But the voice gains in volume and confidence and, as heads turn, the attention grows, like tributaries forming a great river. Soon, David Clark, the normally taciturn Nova Scotian, has the floor, which he won't yield for the next hour, his audience rapt until the end.

A now-retired repairman for the provincial telephone company, David is an Atlantic salmon angler of particular skill. His game was honed on the crowded, competitive, open-to-the-public salmon water in his home province. His precise, quick, no-nonsense casts end up swimming his fly through every possible salmon lie, increasing the odds of a fish actually seeing it, which is all you can really ask for when angling for Atlantics. He doesn't drink or smoke and has a glass of milk with his dinner every night.

He tells the story of a man he ran into one day while he was installing a phone line. The man owned a wolf. A good wolf, the man insisted, but one that had just harassed the neighborhood kids again. David looks at it through the kitchen window. The wolf—fully grown, its hide patchy—is in the backyard tied to a pole. It sulks as it paces to-and-fro, its head cocked below its pointy shoulders. Its hungry eyes are trained on the house.

The man asks if David would do him a favor. Would David shoot it? He begs. The wolf is old, volatile, getting more violent. It would never survive in the wild. There is only one thing to do. Please? It has to be done, but the man can't bring himself to do it. The man loves that wolf.

Shoot it? No way, David thinks. But then he looks into the man's face and sees something wide-eyed and desperate, the look of someone falling. David takes the man's rifle and walks into the backyard and fires. The report is still echoing through the neighborhood when he hears a wail coming from within the house. The wolf lies limp in a pool of its own blood. The man meets David at the door, tears streaming down his red cheeks, grabs the gun, then slams the door in David's face.

Then there's the story about the old lady. David enters a dark, cobwebby house that reeks of sour vinegar. A homely gray woman wears only a thin, tattered nightgown. Too thin. She has no teeth. David is there to fix her phone jack. He's repulsed, barely able to keep his lunch down. He concentrates on the job, on his fingers, which twist and crimp the wires.

She appears behind him and offers a bowl of peanuts. David takes a handful, just to be polite. "These are good," he says, crunching the nuts, trying to hide the surprise of this revelation, given the surroundings.

The old lady looks at David, grinning proudly with her gray gums, and splutters, "You should have tasted them before I sucked off all the chocolate."

END OF THE SEASON

II.

Ernest Long is seventy-six years old. The smile lines on his face give him the beatific look of a wrinkly newborn. Shrapnel in Korea took part of his earlobe. He's missing most of his right heel from a very hard landing during a training jump for a secret airborne mission in Vietnam. He wobbles as he walks.

Ernest has guided on the Miramichi and its tributaries for more than fifty years. Fishing under his tutelage feels, perhaps, like it did to play football for Bear Bryant. Ernest was a friend of Ted Williams's, who once owned a pool on the Miramichi near the town of Blackville. He knew Ted when he was still a fairly young man, fresh off his Hall of Fame baseball career, when he could cast a fly a country mile with exquisite precision. He knew Ted when his body started to break down, when the frustration from not being able to put the fly exactly where he wanted came like a sudden storm, screwing his thin lips into a downward crescent that soured his handsome, leathery face. And he knew Ted when he finally gave up fishing, confined to a wheelchair, a wool blanket draped over his knees and those once-powerful wrists reduced to skinny sticks. Ernest knew all of Ted's wives.

Ernest tells the story of the last time he saw Ted, on one of the great ballplayer's final visits to his beloved water. Ted had invited guests for the weekend, a husband and wife. The couple fished his pool every day. Ted, frail, unwell, sat on the porch and watched—his eyes still keen—mentally cataloging each cast, his wrinkled hands clasped around a cup of tea gone cold.

On the last day of the hot weekend, fishless to that point with the salmon in their midsummer fugue, Ted asked Ernest to wheel him down to the water's edge. Ernest complied, of course. The man and his wife were flailing away again in the pool, all hope of actually catching a fish long gone, but keeping at it out of politeness or perhaps fear. The man seemed to be sweating profusely. He shot nasty glances at his wife, looking for someone to blame for this embarrassment. Ted watched them, eagle-eyed.

"BASTARDS COULDN'T CATCH A FISH IF THEIR LIFE DEPENDED ON IT," Ted said, his voice booming over the riffles.

Ernest thoughtfully stared down at his shoes and said nothing, then wheeled the great ballplayer back up to his house.

III.

Billy Taylor and I are in the canoe with Ernest, who stands in the back and poles us gently down the stream. The Miramichi is high and cold, so we're on the Cains, a little blackwater tributary, sent to scout, to see if its own high water has brought in fish. It's cold. Ernest's old nose drips. "I need some Skroal for my sinuses," he says. I prefer his pronunciation. He takes a pinch and sticks it under his lip.

The Cains is only accessible through miles of unmarked double-track logging roads. We take a four-wheel-drive truck in. When Ernest was younger, he biked the seven wooded miles. He estimates that in his life he's spent nearly a thousand days on this river.

The thick white pines, birches, and maples that crowd the shoreline are second-growth, some even third-growth. They are no less beautiful for it. It's not hard to imagine what this place looked like a century or two ago. The deciduous trees are dressed in their autumn finery, but the big rain year has taken some of the edge off their colors. The leaves smolder but seem to have never quite caught flame. In the breeze, they shudder like peacocks' tails.

Both Billy and I are getting short strikes on our flies. The salmon are here, they are interested, but not yet ready to fully commit. I clip down the tail of my Copper Killer. Billy switches to a Kylie Shrimp pattern with a long-shanked hook. He hooks and lands a pretty eighteen-pound female.

Near the end of the day, at Hopewell Pool, the light goes flat, the stunning mise en scène of the autumnal eventide in Atlantic Canada. The world has gone gold, briefly. I tie on a bright orange Ally's Shrimp and cast over a submerged boulder. As the fly reaches the outside edge of the V-wake, it stops, abruptly. Then the line begins to exit my reel in a startling manner. I wade to the bank, then scramble downstream. Ernest grabs his net and wobbles after me. The fish leaps, its muscled, streamlined body propelled completely out of the water. I forget to bow my rod. The fish stays on anyway. It begins to relent. I reel in as fast as I can. Ernest gets into position below me, calmly murmuring instructions. The big fish nears the net, the Ally's Shrimp in the crook of its kyped jaw. Then it leaps out of the water again, hurdling over the big-mouthed net with a foot to spare. Ernest's cackle echoes through the woods. "Oh, God, I've never seen *that* before," he says, river water dripping from the sleeves of his jacket. The fish turns again and Ernest scoops it up.

IV.

In many ways, Atlantic salmon angling is the most basic form of fly-fishing. Very few times during a salmon angling week will you need a parachute cast or an S-cast. The meat of most salmon days is made of sixty-foot casts made downstream at a forty-five-degree angle with wet flies. In a good pool, with an even, medium-fast flow, you cast, maybe throw in a mend, and then just leave the line alone, letting the current do all the work of tightening your line and swimming your dangling fly over the salmon lies. At the end of the drift, you pull some line in, take a half step downstream, and cast again. All day: step, cast, repeat.

It's the simplest form of fly angling. It can also be the most mysterious. The salmon are not hungry, not driven by the desire to eat. Instead, they strike flies out of some sort of pre-coital aggressiveness, or maybe curiosity, or perhaps from some latent memory of their time spent in this same river as a smolt and a parr, eating mayflies or dace. Sometimes the salmon are in the mood, sometimes they aren't. All of this makes the jolt of the unforgettable take—like shaking hands like an overeager Texan—that much more fulfilling.

You fish slowly, carefully, through each pool, attempting to throw a strike with every cast, to cover every lie and show your fly to every salmon in the pool. You split the day in two, fishing from nine A.M. to one P.M., then take three hours for a lunch with wine. A nap, some reading, perhaps some fiddling with your tackle, then you're out again, on new water, for four more hours in the evening. Resting something, whether it is a pool or an individual fish or even you, is part of the game. When a salmon rises to your fly but doesn't take, the old guide's tale is that you should rest it (i.e., not cast to it) for the amount of time it takes to smoke a cigarette. Since cancer sticks are hard to come by these days, you just stand in the water and wait, left alone with your thoughts, a deafening silence. The wait can be maddening, especially if you were raised a trout angler or an American. You're left to think about how the hell you missed the fish the first time, how big it might be, how you boozed your way through college, why there is an *s* in the word "lisp." Every muscle in your body wants to recast right away. But you fight that temptation. You struggle against your own limitations. Then, finally, you cast.

2009

18

The Lion in Winter

On the Upper West Side of Manhattan, by the hilly riverside park where the great green breast of spring has just begun to reveal itself, I walk into the handsome sixteen-story prewar building and introduce myself to a nattily attired doorman.

"Mr. Lyons is ready for you. Ninth floor."

The *ding* of the elevator, a knock, the door to the apartment opens, and I am greeted by a ninety-two-year-old man, stout and of medium height. Though he had recently described his post-pandemic look as "a badly tied trout fly," his white beard is now neat, his hair obedient. He wears a rose-colored short-sleeved Oxford shirt and blue pants. His gray eyes are full of intelligence and warmth.

A walker stands ready in the vestibule but goes unused as we make our way through the apartment. Bookshelves are everywhere, of course—five by my count—all crammed to capacity. The vibrant watercolors of his late wife adorn the walls of the living room, which faces south and is bathed in sunlight.

There, he settles into a leather couch, and I take an adjacent seat. I've come to talk to him about his life, one of outsized significance in the world of fly-fishing. Because, you see, before *A River Runs Through It*, before Instagram posts and YouTube videos, before podcasts and the pandemic's booming effect, there was Nick Lyons.

In his various roles as a publisher, editor, mentor, and writer, Nick Lyons is, inarguably, one of the most important figures in fly-fishing, the great lion of the sport's literary world, a man who "combined his background of literary cultivation with his personal love of fishing and became a proselytizer of the literature of angling," says Thomas McGuane.

If, in the pre-internet era, one desired practical, how-to information about the sport, or wanted to read works from its best storytellers, one more than likely obtained said things from either Lyons's eponymous publishing house or his pen. "Nick was a major inflection point in the sport of fly-fishing," says Tom Rosenbauer. Adds the author Ted Leeson, "All of fly-fishing publishing coalesced around Nick then. He was the driving force, the epicenter."

Lyons's effect on the sport resonates to this day—"out of old fields comes all the new corn," as Chaucer wrote. He published seminal books on casting and knots, and pioneering ones on flies, strategies, and catching difficult fish, all of which helped the sport evolve and become more accessible. His own essay writing and the many prose stylists he championed—some of whom are still working today—have heavily influenced the new generation of writers. "He basically invented the profession I work in," says John Gierach.

○━◆━○

Lyons was born in Brooklyn in June 1932. His father, an insurance broker, died three months before he was born, so Lyons and his mother went to live with her parents and brothers in the Bronx.

One day, when Lyons was five, his mother told him that they were going on a car trip with one of his uncles. They drove to Westchester County, arriving at a large gabled building, where they were met by a stern-looking woman. The woman asked if Lyons liked playing with toys. When he said yes, she asked him to follow her to a room. Lyons hesitated, glancing back at his mother and uncle. They'll be right there when you return, the woman told him. They were not.

THE LION IN WINTER

The building turned out to be a boarding school run by the stern woman. Lyons spent three years there, "a horrible and dramatic time," he recalls, and never again had a close relationship with his mother. One thing sustained him: a pond on the property filled with sunfish, perch, and bullheads. Lyons fished for them with a branch of ash, a green string, and a hook, and felt, as he would later write, "fully alive" when doing so.

He left the boarding school when he was eight, moving to Brooklyn with his mother and her new husband. He spent his summers then at the Laurel House, a Catskills hotel owned by his grandfather, where he worked, eavesdropped on the conversations of the guests, and fished a nearby lake and creek with worms. Those summers provided a respite from his home life. Lyons never really cared for this stepfather and the feeling was mutual. His stepfather expressed pride in him just once, when Lyons was accepted to the Wharton School of the University of Pennsylvania.

At Wharton, Lyons majored in insurance. He also played basketball, a scrappy five-foot, nine-inch guard who came off the bench. "I do not remember a thing from my insurance courses," he says. "Basketball is what kept me there. I was crazy about the game."

After getting his degree, Lyons went into the army and was sent to Croix-Chapeau, a town in western France. He was ostensibly there to help build a hospital, but the construction never started, so Lyons and his service-mates had plenty of time to kill. Lyons ran the sports activities at the base. His primary endeavor was something else entirely.

Before going to France, Lyons did basic training at Kentucky's Fort Knox. One day, while on leave, he went to Lexington and, at a rummage sale, picked up a copy of *The Hemingway Reader*. Lyons found a bench in a park, opened the book to "Big Two-Hearted River," and began to read. "The day was hot, and I was so intent on the story that when I got back to Fort Knox, I had a welt of sunburn on my ankle," he says. That story, he says, opened something for him. "I sensed that a story about fishing, which was something I loved, could be literature." From that point on, he began to read with intent, carrying paperbacks in the pockets of his army field jacket and feeding "some deep and inchoate hunger."

When he returned to New York from France, he enrolled in literature classes at the New School, reading and writing with great energy and that hunger, but without focus. His teacher there told him, "You're not dumb, Nicki. Just illiterate." This only fueled him. He enrolled—at twenty-five years old—as a freshman at Bard College in upstate New York. There, he read and reread the Great Books. "I fell in love with literature because it contained within it not the answers, but all of the questions," he says. He also fell deeply in love with a fellow student, a frizzy-haired painter named Mari. They married a year later and left Bard to move to Ann Arbor, Michigan, so Lyons could pursue his PhD in English at the university and become, well, literate.

One day while at Michigan, he and Mari went for a drive. They stopped at a bridge over the Au Sable River and watched a man fish with a flyrod. "I knew it was out there, fly-fishing," Lyons says. "I even had a flyrod at UPenn and practiced casting on the basketball court. I never fished with it, though. It was the sight of that guy fishing below the bridge, the use of the fly, the rising trout. I made a mental commitment then."

He later wrote about that first blush of ardor in the *New York Times* in 1985:

> Discovering and rediscovering, fiddling around and practicing, I began to take a few fish. What a sweet and intense madness I relive when I remember those first few years of fly-fishing! It was first love: all heat and heart, no light; all blunder and fumbling, no skill. I couldn't read enough about it. I couldn't resist buying paraphernalia enough for a 10-month safari in trout country, if you had 20 bearers . . . I was addicted, gut-hooked.

After Michigan, Lyons and Mari moved to New York City. He got a job as an English professor at Hunter College, where he would work for the next twenty-six years. "I loved teaching and was very enthusiastic," he says. "I think I was good at showing my students that this wasn't an academic exercise. It was something that could have a real effect on their lives."

Lyons and Mari soon had four children (three sons and a daughter), with just four and a half years separating the oldest from the youngest. Money got tight, so Lyons took a job as a proofreader at Crown Publishing, moving his teaching duties to night classes. He would hold two jobs for the next sixteen years. At one point, he added a third, doing some ghostwritten books, including one on Rose Kennedy that became a bestseller. "I would work at Crown during the day, teach at night until nine, then do my ghostwriting until two in the morning, and then wake up at seven to take the kids to school and then go back to work," says Lyons.

He still found time to fish, an itch he had to scratch, making treks to the Amawalk Reservoir, the branches of the Croton River, or the Catskills. His fishing, though, put a strain on his family, to the point, he says, where he almost lost them. "I was working too much and then I'd go off on a weekend to fish. The kids were in their early teens, the family large and complex, and I'd come back home and Mari, who was usually a shy and quiet person, would be a wreck."

His compulsion to fish sometimes reached the point of absurdity. After one Father's Day lunch, as he and his family were driving home, he stopped at a bridge over the east branch of the Croton, where he saw trout rising. "Mari said, 'Don't be long,'" he says. He rigged up his rod and, lost in the moment, waded into the river in his dress shoes and suit. "It was disastrous for a while," he says. "Two or three times I thought my marriage was over. I once found Mari's wedding ring on top of my tackle satchel." But, eventually, he slowed down a bit, and the kids got older and easier to manage, and Mari began to accompany him on fishing trips and even began to enjoy them, doing plein air paintings.

At Crown, Lyons worked his way up to executive editor. It was there, in the late 1960s, where he began his career as the patron saint of American fly-fishing literature. That year, he acquired the rights to Art Flick's *Streamside Guide*, an essential how-to book that had gone out of print. He talked Orvis into buying 5,000 copies and the book took off. On the strength of its sales, Lyons established the Sportsmen's Classic series, and he obtained the rights to other forgotten classics like Vincent Marinaro's *A Modern Dry-Fly Code* and Sparse Grey Hackle's *Fishless Days* (which Lyons repacked as *Fishless Days, Angling Nights*).

In 1974, Lyons cut out on his own, establishing Nick Lyons Books, an independent publisher that was first a subsidiary of a British concern and then its own entity. (He would later partner with a man named Peter Burford for eight years before going solo again with the Lyons Press.) Lyons continued to seek out classics that had fallen out of favor, but combined that with finding first-time authors like David Quammen and W. D. Wetherell. He published the groundbreaking *Selective Trout* by Doug Swisher and Carl Richards, which has since sold some 200,000 copies, and the pioneering saltwater books *Inshore Fishing* and *Stripers on the Fly* by Lou Tabory. *Practical Fishing Knots*, written by Lefty Kreh and Mark Sosin in 1991, has sold 150,000 copies and is still in print. Lyons talked Rosenbauer into writing *The Orvis Fly-Fishing Guide*, which has since sold around 500,000 copies. ("I owe everything to Nick," says Rosenbauer.) Lyons also published Gierach, Leeson, James Prosek, William Humphrey, Harry Middleton, Flip Pallot, Dave Whitlock, Gary LaFontaine, and Joan and Lee Wulff.

Lyons edited many collections of fishing stories as well, like *Hemingway on Fishing* and *The Best Fishing Stories Ever Told* (which includes pieces by Kreh, Howell Raines, and John McPhee). Later, as he expanded his list to include other outdoor and outdoor-related pursuits, he put out books by McGuane (on horses), Jay McInerney (on wine), Rick Bass (on wolves), and George Plimpton (on sports). In 1992, his house published *Eiger Dreams*, a collection of climbing essays and the first book of a then-relatively unknown young writer named Jon Krakauer. Lyons says he had no idea Krakauer would go on to reach the heights he eventually would. "Back then, I wasn't really looking into the future. I was concentrating on one book at a time. But I knew it was first-rate."

Manuscripts and pitches flooded his office, yet Lyons managed to read nearly every submission that came in, looking for fresh voices. Once,

THE LION IN WINTER

while Lyons was fishing the Yellowstone, a man waded out to him and handed him a manuscript. "I didn't publish that one," he says.

There were perils to being an independent publisher. The low advances meant Lyons missed out on some promising writers. And, oftentimes, a writer would find success with Lyons and then move on to a bigger house, as Krakauer and Quammen did. "That always hurt as an editor, as I spent a lot of time with the authors and their books, getting them out and talking them up," he says. "But, of course, I understood."

One writer who never left Lyons was Leeson, whose first book, *The Habit of Rivers*, was a big success. "Nick is just a terrifically generous and loyal person who works relentlessly for his writers," says Leeson, who went on to write another three books, all done with Lyons or his son, Tony, who took over for his father as the president of the Lyons Press in 1999 until it was sold to Globe Pequot Press in 2001. (Tony now runs Skyhorse Publishing.)

Lyons, of course, cemented his place in the sport of fly-fishing not only as a publisher and editor, but also as a writer himself. After getting his PhD, he wrote critical essays for academic journals and wrote a book about a minor poet for Rutgers University Press. "But I wanted something else, something that used a lot of different parts of myself and that was devoid of all possible attachments to the academic world," he says. He found it through writing about fly-fishing.

One year in the late 1960s, through the *New Yorker* cartoonist Jimmy Mulligan, Lyons met a man named Frank Mele, who was a musician, author, and legendary Catskills angler. The three men decided to fish the Beaverkill River one day, but what was supposed to be an hour-and-a-half trip took nine hours because the "Delphic and hilarious" Mele, as Lyons described him, insisted the trio stop at every bar along the way. When they finally arrived at the river near sunset, neither Lyons nor Mulligan could see straight enough to tie on a fly. Mele, on the other hand, waded in and caught two nice trout.

The next day, Lyons wrote a story about the trip in one sitting. He titled it "Mecca" and sent it to *Field & Stream*, which bought it. Shortly thereafter, he wrote another story for the magazine, this one about gigging a large trout when he was seven years old on the creek that ran by the Laurel House. "I think that second story is when I really found my voice," says Lyons.

He went on to publish eight books about fly-fishing, write outdoor stories for the *New York Times*, and, for twenty-three years starting in 1976, pen "The Seasonable Angler" column on the back page of *Fly Fisherman* magazine. For Lyons, writing and fly-fishing went together because both contained within them a "happy complexity" and a "whole world of different and interesting things."

"I never went fishing without a story attached to it," he says. "That's what interested me the most, not the theories, but the stories. The language of writing about fly-fishing has a warmth, an excitement and a texture to it that other activities don't."

Lyons's writing also had an earthiness and self-deprecation and a lack of pretension to it. "He was really one of the people who cracked open the fly-fishing essay," says Leeson. His prose was casual, measured, and thoughtful, but also exciting in its buildup, the polar opposite of today's social media posts, which threaten to turn the world of fly-fishing into a beauty pageant.

In the three hundred or so stories Lyons wrote about fly-fishing, he often portrayed himself as a bumbler. This, he says, was done by design. "The fishing field had a lot of people pounding their chests at the time. I think not being afraid of making fun of yourself gets you the closest to being a reasonably honest writer."

The funny thing is that those who fished with him rarely, if ever, witnessed a bumbler. "He was a good angler," says Leeson, who spent many days with him on the water. Rosenbauer first fished with Lyons on the upper Willowemoc River. "I expected him to fall in," he says. "But I was blown away by what an athletic caster he was."

So the self-denigrating part was exaggerated a bit? "I had my days," Lyons says with a smile.

THE LION IN WINTER

One of the most influential pieces Lyons ever wrote was also one of his shortest. *Fly Fisherman* sent him a book in galleys, published by the University of Chicago Press. "I liked the title novella immediately and wrote a short—three hundred words or so—but glowing review in the magazine," he says. It was Norman Maclean's *A River Runs Through It*, of course, and Lyons's review, the first of significance, set the book on its blockbuster course.

Some, including his dean at Hunter College, believed Lyons was wasting his vast literary talents by publishing, editing, and writing about fly-fishing. But that literature is important, Lyons says. Its vastness—it's among the most written-about sports in literature—spoke for itself, and the consolidating and curating of that tradition felt like a calling. "The best at it, like McGuane, have added a dimension to the sport, made it more pleasurable," says Lyons. They've inarguably made the lives of many of us more pleasurable, too.

Lyons's last fishing trip was three years ago in Florida, where he cast live shrimp on a spinning rod for bonefish and caught mangrove snappers instead. Being a nonagenarian, he says, comes with some costs. He has a problem now with his balance, which has forced him from the riverbanks and even from boats. "I've taken about a dozen really bad falls and it's just dumb luck that I haven't knocked out an eye or killed myself," he says.

Most of all, he misses the fishing he did on O'Dell Spring Creek in Montana, where he was a frequent guest of the late Herb Wellington, who owned the ranch through which the creek flowed. "It was the best fishing experience I had, on those eight or nine miles that snaked around those fields," Lyons says. "The fishing was so interesting, so demanding at times and, at other times, you couldn't keep them off your line." He particularly loved the brown trout that inhabited the creek. "I liked all trout, but preferred the brown because of the way they took the fly and fought. I loved their coloring. And I loved the way they took positions in the water and held them."

O'Dell's was the fishing spot Mari liked best, too. After Lyons turned over the business to Tony, he and Mari went to O'Dell's a half-dozen times, often spending more than a month there. Mari frequently accompanied him to the creek to paint.

Of course, being a nonagenarian means there's a strong likelihood of enduring other costs, ones that inflict more pain than anything physical ever could. In 2016, after fifty-eight years of marriage to Lyons, Mari died of cancer. Two years later, Lyons's oldest son Paul died of melanoma. "Nick was pretty wrecked after that," says Leeson. Indeed, Lyons's voice catches just a bit and those gray eyes mist when he discusses those two events.

But he has beat on. If anything has kept him going—and kept him mentally acute—it's that voice and the opportunity to use it. In 2020, Lyons published a memoir, *Fire in the Straw*, about his journey to finding and acting upon his passion. (The book's title comes from a line by Thomas Lodge about how fire—or passion—can never be hid in the straw.) It's a project he started "without knowing if I'd be able to ever finish it." But in doing so, he joined the likes of Cormac McCarthy, who published two novels at the age of eighty-eight, and Roger Angell, who wrote essays for the *New Yorker* until he was ninety-nine.

Lyons still writes nearly every day, but no longer about fishing. His last angling piece, about an Atlantic salmon he once caught in a Hudson River tributary (it turned out to be stocked), was published in Peter Kaminsky's 2023 collection, *Catch of a Lifetime*. Instead, Lyons writes regularly for the *Pennsylvania Gazette*, the magazine of his alma mater, UPenn. In a way, this has brought his story full circle. The degree he earned at UPenn, Lyons says, started him on the wrong track, one he eventually corrected when he found literature and then his true voice. But now that degree has provided him with a place to use that voice. In his columns, he has written about a feud he once had with one of his former writers and best friends, William Humphrey. He has written about what it's like to turn ninety and about the limits of willpower. And he has written about the grief of losing Mari and Paul and about finding love again with his companion, Ruth, with whom he now lives,

THE LION IN WINTER

and how, in a sense, this late-in-life love has not diminished, but rather enhanced the loves that came before it:

> The loss of Mari, whom I had loved so deeply, brought pain that never ended. I live with her paintings and Paul's essays etched into my brain, and my new life never thinks to let them go. Sometimes I call Ruth "Mari" but she, channeling the great wisdom of the East and gurus who encouraged her to become the person she is, never looks the other way as if waiting for those old loves to fade. We each of us had what we had. It was ours. It gave us life. Now we give each other life, and she helps those loves for Mari and Paul flourish.

Lyons has written eighteen essays for the *Gazette* thus far, and has no plans to stop anytime soon. "I love working on them, fussing around with them," he says. "I just love to write. I'm crazy about it and so grateful for it."

That fire in the straw still burns, brightly.

2024

19

Green Drakes

It was early June and I was on the main stem of the Delaware again, an annual habit that had, decades ago, careened into an addiction. The solstice was nigh, meaning I didn't feel insane for staying on the water and casting a fly until 9:30 P.M. or so. There are a multitude of hatches this time of year that reliably bring up trout—the early morning blue-winged olives, the caddis, and, of course, the most reliable of them all, the yellow-bodied, white-winged sulphurs. But I was here on this broad, open pool on this grand river, watching the sun drop behind the ancient mountains that line its course, because of the Green Drake, *the* mayfly that brings up the largest and orneriest trout of the year.

But the Green Drake hatch in the Catskills occupies a strange liminal zone. It is part reality and part myth—unreliable, unseen by many, predicated on faith. Hardcores who religiously chase the hatch view it in the same way a certain faction of theologians interprets parts of the Old Testament, like the evil snake in the Garden of Eden, the Tower of Babel, and the Great Flood: not as literal stories, but as "profoundly true."

After mating, the Green Drakes sometimes fall from the sky to the water—their bodies morphed into the shape of a cross in an easy-to-see white—and then are eagerly snatched off the surface by big trout. Sometimes, though, they don't fall at all. But that's okay. Even the prospect of a Green Drake spinner fall *maybe* happening is enough for me to drop all appointments, drive up, and allow myself to become wholly absorbed in this land of rivers in southwestern New York.

＊

When I moved to the city for a job a few decades ago, I thought I was done for, that some integral part of my very being was about to be forever interred by the concrete. I spent most of my childhood in the woods and on the waters of Alabama, North Carolina, and Virginia. In Gotham, that life appeared to be over and done with, sacrificed at the altar of a budding career, a steady salary, a group healthcare plan, and a 401k.

But then I discovered the Catskills, just a few hours away from the city by car but eons away in its essence. The rivers that sluiced through the cleavage of the Catskill Mountains—the Beaverkill, Willowemoc, Neversink, Espous, Schoharie, and the east and west branches and the main stem of the Delaware—were loaded not only with trout, but also with history, the water on which modern fly-fishing techniques were pioneered by the likes of Theodore Gordon, Sparse Grey Hackle, Edward Hewitt, Arnold Gingrich, Art Flick, and Lee and Joan Wulff.

In the Catskills, I found immediate and nearly insatiable love. The rivers are gorgeous, cold, and clear. The fish—mainly wild browns and rainbows—are enthralling, large, and very hard to fool. The best anglers on the rivers are like the best East Coast skiers—sharpened by the less-than-perfect conditions, the opposite of what's usually found in the more clement American West. Parts of the Catskills area, especially low on the main stem of the Delaware, remind me of my childhood in the South, with lush green hills, long summer nights, lack of citified hurry, and the hint of backwoods menace—of moonshiners and the distant sound of target practice. There's a dreaminess to the Catskills, a mood that hangs like early morning riversmoke. It all feels like a piece of home.

2023

Andy Mill, Florida Keys.
Photo by the author.

Andros Island,
Bahamas.
Photo by Matt Benson.

Secret bonefish flat, Bahamas.
Photo by the author.

BELOW: Captain Frank Crescitelli and the author.
Photo by Jack Reynolds.

ABOVE: New York Harbor. *Photo by Jack Reynolds.*
BELOW: Upper Delaware River, New York. *Photo by the author.*

ABOVE: Letort Spring Run, Pennsylvania. *Photo by the author.*
BELOW: The author with his daughters. Upper Delaware River, New York. *Photo by Amy Bucher.*

ABOVE: Pathway to a salmon pool, Margaree River, Nova Scotia. *Photo by the author.*
LEFT: Salmon leap, Margaree River, Nova Scotia. *Photo by Ed McCarthy.*

Lake Tadpole, Alabama. *Photo by Dylan Burke.*

ABOVE: John O'Hearn (left) and Nathaniel Linville, Key West, Florida. *Photo by the author.*
RIGHT: Steve Huff, Everglades National Park, Florida. *Photo by David Mangum.*
BELOW: Tarpon hole, Florida Keys. *Photo by Tom Rosenbauer.*

Sebastian Letelier (left) and William Hereford, Chile. *Photo by the author.*

Motorcycle dog, Brooklyn. *Photo by the author.*

20

Sulphurs

Look, I don't want to be dismissive of the other great hatches here in the Northeast. I mean, the Quills—the Gordons, the Blues, the Blacks—are really cool flies with names that have an aristocratic gravitas. (A "Mr. Quill Gordon" will have male descendants with "Jr." and "III" attached to the end of their names. Count on it.) Hendricksons herald the beginning of the season's fun. I like March Browns, even though they appear in May. (They were forever called Grey Foxes until some nerdy entomologists got in the way.) It's nice of the *Isonychias* to hatch, sporadically, all summer long and into the fall. And the meaty Green and Brown Drakes have a way of sometimes making those prudish big-shouldered browns shed their inhibitions about feeding on the surface. Hell, I even like tricos, those tiny, trying, midsummer bastards that can drive an otherwise sane man to golf.

But let's face it. In the East, there is one preeminent mayfly: that white-winged, yellow-bodied beauty known as the sulphur. No other bug on the right coast comes close to its ubiquity. The sulphur plays a part in a nearly perfect, almost Buddhist, continuously looped conditional:

If a stream in the East has trout in it, it more than likely has a sulphur hatch.

If a stream in the East has a sulphur hatch, it more than likely has trout in it.

It's the staple, maize to Mexicans, rice to Chinese, red wine to Italians, high-fructose corn syrup to Americans. Spell it anyway you please: "sulphur" or "sulfur" or even "sulfer." The trout don't give a phuck.

In fact, they seem to prefer the sulphur to any other mayfly. On countless evenings I've waded the Upper Delaware River and watched literally hundreds of Coffin Flies fall to the water, seemingly bringing every trout in the river to the top. Without fail, I will tie on a size-ten Coffin Fly and make fifty casts that are refused by every nose in the pool before I finally tie on a size-fourteen sulphur, to imitate the concurrent hatch, and finally get some takes. It seems to defy logic: the trout are essentially ignoring an unbutton-the-top-of-your-pants meal for a handful of peanuts. Sulphurs must simply taste better. (I can report from firsthand knowledge that, to humans anyway, they taste like a blade of grass with subtle hints of earwax.)

Familiarity certainly plays a significant role in this dietary decision. Sulphurs begin hatching on the Upper Delaware in the late spring. At dusk, just as the river has begun to darken, the retiring sunlight catches their upright wings just so, making them seem to glow, like cigarette lighters held up during the slow song at a hair band concert. It goes on like this for another three months on this river.

On the Letort Spring Run, the books and charts all say that the meat of the sulphur hatch is in late May and June. Fair enough. But the sulphurs never really seem to stop hatching all year. I've fished to a hatch in the welcoming cool of an evening following a brutal hundred-degree August day. A few years ago, I fished a brief but heavy hatch during a snow shower at midday on Christmas Eve.

Sulphurs are incredibly hardy, nearly impervious to the insults of man, a manifestation of the promise of redemption. They are pretty much the only significant mayfly on the ravaged Letort. They were the first mayflies to reappear on both Pennsylvania's Little Juniata River and Spring Creek after chemical spills killed everything in those waters.

SULPHURS

Paul Weamer, the author, fishing guide, and bug dweeb, tells me there are actually two kinds of sulphurs: the "big" sulphur—*Ephemerella invaria*—and the "little" sulphur—*Ephemerella dorothea dorothea* (that second *dorothea* is for those of you who didn't get it the first time). They are sort of related to Hendricksons (they're both *Ephemerella*). But they are not related to Yellow Drakes, cahills, or *Leucrocuta hebes*, or to any of the other myriad mayflies that sport a hint of yellow and white, all bugs some obstinate old-timers call "sulphurs" for simplicity's sake.

It's all good, though. There's plenty of room under the sulphur tent for both entomologists with their suitcases of flies hanging from their chests and the generalists who carry only "light" and "dark" flies in sizes 10–18 in a weathered fly wallet. They all catch fish during the reliable, redemptive hatch of the mayfly known as the sulphur.

2010

21

Thought Rods

To Tom Morgan, the perfect fly rod is a "thought rod." It enables the caster to deliver the fly to a precise spot without being conscious of exactly how they got it there. The rod works intuitively—the way you do when you "think" to shake a hand, pick up a fork, or wave hello. "It should feel like an extension of your body," says Morgan.

In his case, the thought rod metaphor takes on another meaning. Considered by many to be the world's finest living fly rod-maker—a craft that relies almost solely on tangible feel—the sixty-seven-year-old Morgan has not been able to cast, or even hold, one of his creations for more than a decade.

Morgan has multiple sclerosis, a still mystifying degenerative disease that occurs when a mix-up in nerve signal transmissions causes the immune system to attack the insulating sheaths around the nerves. Morgan has a particularly debilitating form of MS and extremely limited movement below his neck. He is confined to his bed and to a high-tech wheelchair with a headrest, a reclining contraption that resembles a dental examination chair. Morgan's thought rods are a pure extension of his mind.

On a sun-sweet summer day, I visit Morgan at his home outside of Bozeman in southwestern Montana, an area veined with some of the best trout rivers in the world. His house doubles as the headquarters of his company, Tom Morgan Rodsmiths. To the west glitters the snowcapped peaks of the Tobacco Root Mountains; to the south lie the grazing lands occupied by Ted Turner's bison herd.

When I arrive, I meet a Morgan client and his wife who have traveled here from Oregon. The man already owns four Morgan rods and is here to test out a fifth. He has a wide-eyed, happy look on his face, like King Arthur on a long-deferred visit to Excalibur's forge. Morgan gets visitors all year-round—pilgrims, really—from as far away as Japan, who come by to cast a rod and put their names on the two-year waiting list to buy one.

After the couple leaves, I walk into the dining area of the house, where Morgan sits in his chair, reclining. His face is weathered from years spent in the Montana sun. He wears big, wide-lensed glasses fitted with two little mirrored squares, known as prism glasses, which allow him to be semirecumbent and still see the person he is talking to. They reflect his eyes, little pools of blue.

By his side is Gerri Carlson, his wife and the co-owner of the company. She periodically puts a straw to his lips so he can sip from a can of Mountain Dew. Carlson, fifty-eight, bright-eyed, and cheerful, is the bridge between Morgan's mind and the making of the rods.

<hr>

Morgan was born in Hollywood, California. In 1946, when his brother's asthma necessitated a move, his parents chose the ranching town of Ennis, Montana, where they opened El Western, a fishing resort. By the age of fifteen, Morgan was a guide, and he spent fourteen years wading beside his clients, observing how their equipment either helped or hindered them. Sometime around 1969, he made his first fly rod.

In 1973, Morgan learned that San Francisco's R. L. Winston Company, one of the hallowed brands in fly rod manufacture, was for sale. Partnering with businessman Sid Eliason, Morgan rustled up the

THOUGHT RODS   119

$110,000 necessary to buy the company and moved it to Twin Bridges, Montana.

Morgan made his first mark as a bamboo rod-maker at Winston, creating rods in the tradition of the nineteenth-century American master H. L. Leonard. In the fly-fishing world, bamboo rods are an enduring foundation, and Morgan mastered this old art.

At first, he primarily made those bamboo rods, along with some constructed of fiberglass. Then, in the early 1970s, graphite hit the scene. By making rods lighter and stiffer, the new material yielded a faster "action"—the bend and speed generated by the rod. Graphite also changed the nature of the business. Every few years a new generation of graphite was introduced in pursuit of what had become the fly-fishing grail: allowing flies to be cast farther and farther. By doing this, rod-makers shrewdly appealed to the way most fishermen road test a rod: in a fly shop parking lot, where, inevitably, they try to cast as far as they can.

But something was lost along the way—finesse. For most types of fly-fishing (especially trout fishing), casting a fly into the next county does not make you a better angler. Most fly-fishing takes place twenty to fifty feet from the caster. Accuracy is the key.

Morgan has dedicated his rod-building life to rods that find that sweet spot. He embraced graphite yet created a rod with a bamboolike, traditional feel. In the mid-1980s, he developed an eight-foot, four-weight rod for Winston—known as the Tom Morgan Favorite—that is "the Coca-Cola of fly rods, what all other rods are measured against," says Jerry Kustich, a fellow rod-maker. (Winston still sells it. Imagine Rossignol still selling skis from the 1980s.)

Morgan never really understood the fetish with distance casting, yet it was apparently what fly fishermen wanted. The trend was among the reasons—along with financial incentives—that led him to sell Winston in 1991. "I felt I could make better rods on my own," he says.

He signed a seven-year noncompete clause with Winston and planned to use the years to refresh his mind and work on new designs. But around this time, he felt the first signs that something was amiss with his body. He was in Washington, DC, touring the monuments in what should have been, literally, a walk in the park for an outdoorsman like Morgan. But after a quarter of a mile, he had to sit to rest his legs.

Morgan had episodes like this for the next few months. He would suddenly stumble in a small stream he had fished all his life, and he lost his balance when walking, "like a man who was dizzy or had had too much to drink," says Glenn Brackett, a former partner at Winston. Finally, in 1992, a neurologist in Great Falls diagnosed him with MS.

For a few years, he had what's known as "relapsing-remitting" multiple sclerosis. "There were long stretches when I felt like nothing was wrong with me," Morgan says. It was during this time that he met Gerri Carlson, a former English teacher who had just returned to Montana after a stint in the Peace Corps. At the urging of a friend, she went out with Morgan on a blind date. "I knew nothing of his fame in the fly-fishing world," she says.

In 1995 Morgan suffered a five-month period of near-total collapse. He lost the ability to walk, then the movement in his arms. Facing a raft of medical bills and uncertainty about the future, Morgan petitioned David Ondaatje, the owner of Winston, to release him from the noncompete clause. Ondaatje gave his assent. That allowed Morgan to start Tom Morgan Rodsmiths in 1996. At that point, Morgan was unable to cast a rod from his wheelchair and needed twenty-four-hour care. "We didn't plan it like this," says Carlson. "It just turned out this way." They were married in 1996.

One can't help but listen for a hint of wistfulness in her voice, the leaky crack in a dam holding back a reservoir of regret or resentment. I don't hear it. Neither have others. "I was devastated when I heard how bad things had gotten for Tom and Gerri," says Brackett. "But they never were."

Then came the hard part. In order to make the company work, Morgan had to somehow transmit all his knowledge to Carlson. She was an accomplished quilter, so she had the required nimble fingers. Growing up, she had helped her father, who was a logger, so she was comfortable with heavy tools. But she knew nothing about fly rods or handling graphite blanks.

THOUGHT RODS 121

It is the blanks, the graphite tubes, that are the foundation of a Morgan's exquisite feel—that weightless sensation one experiences with, say, a perfectly struck three-iron. Morgan had his recipe for the blanks, which were manufactured under a veil of secrecy at G. Loomis, a Washington State fly rod company owned by friends, stored on his voice-activated computer. (Mounted on a swinging arm over his hospital bed, the computer is Morgan's gateway to the world: he reads books and trades stocks with it, and estimates he's sent 19,000 emails in the last decade.) He had fiddled for years with the taper of the blanks to get the bend that would load best with twenty to fifty feet of line. Morgan's blanks, when made into rods, actually store energy in the bend, so that in a forward cast, the rod, not the wrist, does most of the work.

Morgan could still handle quality control, running his experienced eye over the blanks when they came in. (Half don't meet his demanding standards in flex or aesthetics.) But somehow he had to impart to Carlson the other crucial aspects of fly rod-making: the wrapping of the guides, the application of the finish, and the turning of the cork handles. Early on, Morgan tried to explain how to make a jig for drilling cork. It took her all day to do a task that would have taken Morgan an hour or so to complete, leaving her exhausted and frustrated. "I would be lying in bed at 5:30, just wiped out from the day in the shop. And I'd still have to make dinner," she says.

One of the problems was that Morgan tried to micromanage the process, detailing it step-by-step, envisioning Carlson as merely the hands of the operation. "But I needed to be more than that. I needed to get into the creative process," she says. After a day on which they both ended up in tears, Morgan changed his methods, focusing on helping her understand the final product and letting her develop her own methods of getting there. He would describe a step as many times as needed for her to "get it," then back off. It turned out that nimble fingers and comfort with tools aside, the patience that Carlson had acquired as an English teacher was her best preparation for the task—astonishingly, she gained proficiency in only a few months.

When Morgan's fishing buddies came by to test the new rods, they discovered something remarkable: "Tom's Winston rods were some of the best ever made," says George Anderson, owner of the Yellowstone Angler in Livingston, Montana. "But these were better."

Morgan and Carlson make thirty-five to forty graphite rods a year, in two to six weights, costing up to $1,295. Morgan recently added a line of bamboo rods that are as fine as any on the market. They sell twenty a year for $3,850 a pop. I own one of Morgan's Winston rods and count it among my most prized possessions. But casting his latest models made me feel like that guy from Oregon. The seven-foot, four-weight bamboo is the perfect marriage of ancient form and modern function. The eight-and-a-half-foot, five-weight graphite model has a sweet and smooth action, progressing without a knock or hitch from the strong butt to the soft and supple tip. That sensitive tip allows for accuracy in closer casts; the stiff butt means you can crank out a long one when needed. The feel of a Morgan rod—which is personal and hard to describe, a bit like love—lulls the user, when on the stream, into what novelist Vance Bourjaily once called "the trance of instinct."

The unparalleled beauty of his rods is easier to put into words. They have a rich garnet varnish and reel seats made from exotic woods, like beautifully burled amboyna. The looping cursive script on the butt and the octagonal rod tube add to the delight.

Morgan, with the considerable help of Carlson, has accomplished something similar to Beethoven, who, late in his life, went completely deaf, losing what he called "my most prized possession," only to compose arguably his finest works. Morgan is a composer too, creating something meant for others to play. That, according to Carlson, has saved his life.

2008

22

December

For six years straight, I made a trip to fish the Letort Spring Run in December, squeezing in one last day on what was, at the time, my favorite water in the world. I was obsessed with the place—its history, its beauty, its tenuousness. Other anglers came to the Letort and fished it as a one-off ceremony, making a token cast, taking pictures of the Cooperstown-like plaques of Vincent Marinaro and Charlie Fox mounted in its meadows, and then high-tailing it out of there for more productive water.

I fished it like it was the last trout stream in the world. In the spring, I would leave work at six P.M., embarking on a four-hour round-trip drive just to catch the last half hour of the sulphur hatch. In the summer, I sweated through hundred-degree middays, slowly edging my way through the chest-high grasses to get into position to cast a beetle tight to the banks, just underneath the dapping willow branches. The Letort was my refuge, and never more so than during the year's final month, that period of time often accompanied by the vague uneasiness caused by the mix of darkness and excess.

That refuge would turn out to be fleeting.

On my final trip to the Letort, I walked upstream, deliberately avoiding my favorite stretch of the creek in the meadow named after Marinaro. It was noon on Christmas Eve. I paced the banks, trying to stay warm, cursing the uselessness of fingerless gloves. The Letort's exquisite water moved before me, sprung from the earth as limpid and thick-looking as baby oil, its surface etched by microcurrents. Watercress—still bright green because of the creek's stable temperatures—swayed rhythmically under the water.

At around two P.M., it started to snow. Only a few flakes appeared at first, indecisively zigzagging their way out of the gray sky. But within minutes, the flurries became a full-blown storm, producing that type of whiteout that provides the sense of utter solitude.

Speaking generally, fishing for *salmonids* in Pennsylvania in December on any river that does not empty into Lake Erie is foolish. Truth be told, the Letort is a bitch to fish even during prime mayfly season—there aren't many fish in the creek and those that do live there are extremely anxious about their wellbeing.

But I was infatuated by the Letort, dreaming about it by day, and fishing through its runs in my head at night when I couldn't sleep. Which is why I could not bring myself to go to Marinaro's on this Christmas Eve. Not yet, anyway.

I was in Otto's Meadow instead, the section of the creek where the irascible Eddie Shenk—for four decades the Letort's most creative and determined angler—had landed a ten-pound brown in the 1980s, the creek's last great fish. In the midst of the snowstorm, I noticed something on the water. Dimples. Up and down the creek, the fish were gulping the little white flakes that were landing on the water and *not* melting. It was a sulphur hatch. I started to cast through the falling snow. I caught two browns, the biggest maybe twelve inches. The hatch was over in twenty minutes. The day's light began to fail.

⚬—⚬

I finally mustered the will to make the walk down to Marinaro's. The Letort had faced perils before. A pesticide spill had once killed most of

DECEMBER 125

its trout and mayflies. At the bottom of Marinaro's was a bridge for Interstate 81, bearing trucks whose downshifts sounded like human groans. The creek had survived these blights, emerging weaker, but still alive.

There was a sense, however, that the Home Depot under construction on the bank across from Marinaro's might be the knockout blow, if not for the fish, then certainly for the creek's soul.

The town leaders had wooed the chain, crowing about increased tax revenues. "Progress," they called it.

I had sent a check to the undermanned resistance at the local Trout Unlimited chapter. I had written a letter to the corporation, pleading with them to place the store pretty much anywhere else. But I knew even as I was doing these things that they were futile, a butter knife brought to a gunfight.

I stood in Marinaro's and stared across the creek at the massive parking lot that had just been finished and thought about how pavement is forever. It was dark now. The streetlamps surrounding the lot glowed, aureoled by the storm. My face was stinging and wet from the snow. I walked back to my car and took down my rod with numbed fingers. There are 2,300 Home Depots in the world. There is only one Letort.

2010

23

Second-Chance Trout

On our second night at Cinco Rios Lodge in southern Chile, Sebastian Galilea, the lodge's enthusiastic forty-six-year-old majority owner, tells us the story of the "lost grape of Bordeaux." The Carménère, he explains, originally grew in Bordeaux as one of the region's foundational grapes. Winemakers used it to produce a coveted varietal, a medium-bodied red with a certain zest that, to many oenophiles, elevated it above similar wines, like merlot.

In 1867, though, catastrophe struck. A plague of phylloxera—a grape-destroying insect—decimated the Carménère grape in Bordeaux. Attempts to replant it failed. Carménère wine, it was believed, had gone extinct.

Then in 1994, a noted French expert in cultivated grapes, Jean-Michel Boursiquot, came to Chile to take part in a wine symposium. In his free time, he visited a local vineyard. There, he spotted a small triangular plot of vines labeled as merlot. He took a closer look—the shape of the leaves and the flower stamens reminded him of something else, a grape he'd seen only in a university collection of extinct varieties.

And here, Galilea pauses his story. He grabs a bottle of red wine, uncorks it and pours a glass.

"And guess what?" he says, taking a sip. "It was the Carménère!"

The grapes had apparently arrived in Chile sometime in the mid-nineteenth century and been sold there for more than a century as a merlot. Now the country is the largest producer of Carménère in the world.

It wasn't the only time that a foreign import thrived in this land of second chances.

We are here, the twelve of us—nine guests, whose occupations range from a judge to a microbiologist, along with our host, Orvis's Tom Rosenbauer, the photographer William Hereford, and me—on a weeklong trip split between two lodges. Both are owned by Galilea and his partner, the Welshman Greg Vincent: Cinco Rios, located in the temperate rainforest on the banks of the Simpson River, near the charming town of Coyhaique; and Estancia del Zorro, some twenty-five miles to the northeast, up in the mountain pampas grasslands near the border of Argentina.

Galilea and Vincent used to operate the two lodges as separate entities. But thanks to a suggestion from a client fifteen years ago, they now divide the week between them, which means guests have access to nineteen freestone rivers, six spring creeks, more than a dozen lakes and lagoons, and countless small streams. The idea is that you, the angler, can experience the full breadth of trout fishing in Patagonia. And, well, this movable fishing feast delivers.

During the week at Cinco Rios and del Zorro, you can fish a hatch, chuck a streamer from a raft, fish a hopper, fish a hopper with a dropper nymph, fish a technical spring creek, fish an untechnical spring creek, fish riffles or pastoral pools, fish a lake, cast into a creek no wider than the length of your boot, cast into a river as broad as the Yellowstone, and even fish on the other side of the Continental Divide in Argentina. The only frustration: it's impossible to do it all.

The trip is a slice of trout-fishing nirvana. The resource is treated with care—anglers are spread out and rotated among the vast offerings, and much of the water gets "rested" for days, ensuring un-hassled fish. If you, like me, have become a bit disheartened by the state of trout fishing in

SECOND-CHANCE TROUT

129

North America—with its maddening crowds, ruthlessly efficient methods (i.e., the vacuum-like practice of Euro-nymphing), hook-scarred fish, and constant stream of Instagram grip-and-grin posts, all of which diminish rather than enhance the sport—this is a place you can go to rediscover the soul of something that seems to have been lost . . . with fish that weren't even here until 150 years ago.

On our first day at Cinco Rios, Hereford and I get paired with the guide Carlos Andrade, an irrepressible forty-six-year-old ball of joy with a long black beard that he braids and, on occasion, serves as a repository for used flies. We fish the middle section of the Simpson River, a medium-sized waterway with big, slow, willow-lined pools tinted green. Andrade attaches a large yellow-bodied, white-winged stonefly to the end of our lines, with a small nymph dropped off, and we cast as close as we dare to the overhanging willows that serve as trout cover. While little fish prefer the nymph, the dry fly attracts big browns and rainbows, which average around eighteen inches in length. It is a day on which every blind cast, as Hereford points out, is done with the hope—almost the expectation—that a big trout will rise for the fly. And if one doesn't, well, there's always the next one.

At midday, Andrade lays out a red-and-white checked tablecloth for lunch in a field of purple lupine and slipper-like yellow capachito flowers, producing a charcuterie plate and chicken paella, which we wash down with sips of Carménère. The sun is high, the breeze light. It is as easygoing a fishing day as I can remember.

The next day, again with Andrade, we move farther up the Simpson, this time accompanied by Tom Larsen, a retired lawyer from San Francisco whose mind is a fecund storehouse of ideas for everything from education reform to potential movie scripts. A dirt road takes us through the rolling green valley by small farms guarded by tall rows of fast-growing, wind-breaking alamos trees. We pass a few gauchos, all on horseback and trailed by herding dogs. The gauchos stop to watch us bounce by. A look into their weather-beaten faces provides the sensation of having have been borne back centuries.

The Simpson in this upper section would look familiar to anyone who has fished the freestone rivers of the western US—gone are the slow green pools, replaced by knee-deep riffles and runs and the occasional bend pool, backdropped by dramatic mountain peaks. We fish a brief but exciting mayfly hatch, then throw hoppers and droppers in the runs and riffles, again catching more than our fill of good-sized trout.

At some point in the morning, a commotion occurs near my legs, as if someone has tossed a few fist-sized rocks into the river, kicking up a wall of water. I look down and see, slowly swimming away from me, a three-foot-long fish that I had spooked.

"King salmon," Andrade tells me.

King salmon? "Do you guys ever fish for them?" I ask, suddenly feeling the familiar rush of fixation taking root.

Andrade explains the salmon are plentiful—and fresh from the sea—on the lower stretches of the Simpson and in the Aysén River, which is formed by the confluence of the Simpson and the Mañihuales Rivers. The fish, the progeny of aquaculture escapees, established themselves as a wild spawning population decades ago. A guide at Cinco Rios knows how to catch them, he tells me. Would I want to try?

The next morning, Hereford and I find ourselves in a white Chinese-made pickup truck towing a jetboat with our guide, Max Safian, a thirty-nine-year-old santiaguino who spends four months of the year away from his job as an artist in the capital city to guide for Cinco Rios. As we wind our way along the lower Simpson River canyon, Safian sings along to the 1990s hip-hop playing through the truck's speakers, songs, he says, that have helped him refine his English. (The guides at Cinco Rios and del Zorro like to curate their drive-time Spotify playlists and try to pair them, like wines, with their anglers for the day. Hereford and I later decide we must have been tough to pin down: during various rides, along with hip-hop, we are treated to classic rock, old-school honky-tonk, and Justin Bieber.)

SECOND-CHANCE TROUT

We arrive at the Aysén, a wide and deep river the color of a Heineken bottle, and launch the boat a mere twenty miles from the Pacific. Safian says he loves salmon and would like to take guests out more often for them, but he doesn't have many takers. Indeed, salmon angling is not a sport for everyone. The rods and lines are heavy (I am using a 350-grain sink tip that has all the levity of a wet mop), and one has to have the right disposition—i.e., be okay with not getting a nibble for hours, days, or sometimes weeks at a time. (The salmon do not eat on their spawning journeys upriver; they hit flies out of instinct or annoyance.) Fishing for salmon here also means voluntarily sacrificing a day away from some of the best trout fishing in the world. But for those who love it—or for natural-born gamblers—the payoff, if it comes, makes it all worth it.

Safian eventually holds the boat in the current and I begin to fish. Not more than twenty casts in, there is a flash of bright silver and my line comes tight. Fifteen minutes later, Safian has in his grip what he says is a twenty-pound King, or Chinook, salmon. After a quick photo session, she kicks off, returning to her river journey. I cast nonstop for the rest of the day, as dozens upon dozens of salmon leap and cavort about the pools, but never get another touch. Still, I leave the river feeling happy and lucky.

That evening, we load into a van and embark on the forty-five-minute trip to Estancia del Zorro (Ranch of the Fox), which has been in Galilea's family as a sheep farm for decades. The charmingly rustic lodge's rooms have been fashioned out of the original, blood-red ranch house, built in 1917. The beds are made with clothesline-dried sheets. A woodstove heats the main room, which also offers a well-stocked bar, comfortable couches for post-fishing tales and pisco sours, and a huge main table for a continuation of the excellent dinners we've had at Cinco Rios, which feature fresh fish, wild morels, and local chicken, lamb, and beef, as well as, on two nights, morsels of Rosenbauer's homemade dark chocolate, which he brought down from Vermont.

Del Zorro itself encompasses fifteen thousand acres, but through lease agreements with his neighbors, Galilea has secured a total of 290,000 acres through which flow six world-class spring creeks filled with giant brown trout, two freestone rivers, a handful of lakes, and some water in nearby Argentina. (To fish there, you hand over your passport at the border and then retrieve it on the way back to the lodge.) I ask Galilea if he knew how the trout got into these high plains spring creeks. He tells me he doesn't, but documentation confirms that as far back as the 1930s, shepherds on the ranch would sometimes snare a trout for a meal in the field.

If geography is indeed destiny, Chile was fated to be a bit of an oddball. The country borders Peru and Bolivia to the north, then Argentina all the way down to the archipelago of Tierra del Fuego in the far south, a thin slice of land nearly three thousand miles in length but only a hundred miles, on average, in width, hemmed in by the still-growing and occasionally volcanic Andes to the east and the cold blue waters of the Pacific Ocean to the west. "We think we are a country," the Chilean poet Nicanor Parra once wrote. "But, actually, we are a landscape at best." The arid Atacama Desert dominates the country in the north, but starting roughly in Santiago and extending all the way down to Tierra del Fuego, Chile is rich in cold and clear rivers, streams, and lakes.

Though gaps exist in the record, the first real planting of trout in Chile is believed to have taken place at the turn of the twentieth century, an effort spearheaded by a German immigrant named Federico Albert Taupp, a conservationist who recognized the country for what it was (it is said of Chile that God created the perfect habitat for trout . . . but just forgot the trout). Taupp had four hundred thousand eggs of brown and rainbow trout and Atlantic salmon, along with some fingerlings, shipped from Hamburg to Valparaíso, Chile, by way of Cape Horn. Only the trout eggs survived, but with that initial stocking—done by rail and horseback—along with some later help from the Chilean government, Man accomplished what God had not. Now, in certain parts of the country, trout represent 80 percent of the biomass in some rivers, and

SECOND-CHANCE TROUT

the nonnative species have become wild. (The effect of trout on Chile's native fish species, according to many studies, is inconclusive.)

For a long while, the white heat of Chilean trout fishing was concentrated in what is, roughly speaking, the middle of the country, from Santiago down to Puerto Montt, mostly because of accessibility. But with the opening of the Carretera Austral—a 770-mile-long road built by the dictator Augusto Pinochet in the late 1980s that connects the north to the south—some of the best fishing in the country is now centered four hundred miles south of Puerto Montt, in the Aysén Region, which has as its hub the town of Coyhaique.

Hereford and I are leaving a day earlier than the rest of the group, so we make the most of our two days at del Zorro. On day one, we join Rosenbauer and Hector Cuell, a mellow, thirty-four-year-old guide, and drive through the vast expanse of the Valley of the Moon, with its crater-like mounds surrounded by rising hills that look like wrinkled brown elephant hides. We pass spring ponds filled with floating birds: torrent ducks, black-necked and white-bodied swans, Andean geese, and Technicolor pink flamingos. Darwin's rheas—a flightless bird that looks like a small ostrich—scoot through the pampas grass, spooked by our presence.

We first stop at one of the most remarkable trout streams I've ever seen—a creek, if you could call it that, no more than a foot-and-a-half wide in some places. "Oh, *yeah*," Rosenbauer says as he lays eyes on it. Rosenbauer is a particular fan of small trout creeks, but even *he* hasn't fished anything like this.

Rosenbauer, white whiskered with big blue eyes often widened in wonderment, is a forty-nine-year Orvis veteran who, through his popular podcast, his twenty-plus books, and his general advocacy, has become, arguably, the most prominent face in the sport of fly-fishing. (This despite the fact that his fans sometimes have some trouble with his name—one member of the group was overheard on the plane ride down telling everyone he saw that he was going on a trip with the famous fly fisherman "Tom Rosenhauer.")

Rosenbauer's title at Orvis is, fittingly, "Chief Enthusiast." There is an entire subgenre of Instagram and Reddit posts dedicated to memes about him. He has a sparkle dun fly—his favorite for trout—tattooed on the inside of his left forearm, paired with a bonefish fly on his right one. There is no one I know who is more into fly-fishing and, in particular, fly-fishing for trout. At age seventy, he shows no signs of slowing down.

A big part of his enthusiasm manifests through the teaching of a sport that can seem, at first, a bit intimidating. Within hours of first arriving on the trip, Rosenbauer held an impromptu casting lesson for the group in a field in front of Cinco Rios. "You don't want to do all of that rigid *A River Runs Through It* stuff," he told us as he demonstrated a cast. "You wanna be loose."

Rosenbauer is the first out of the car when we reach the tiny spring creek—if he were a dog, his tail would be wagging—and he quickly rigs up his rod, the fourth generation of Orvis's Helios model, which he and I are gleefully testing this week. Cuell tells us that the stream is named Truchón (big trout) Creek, and we quickly find out why. The fishing consists of casting just your stout, ten-pound leader and a few feet of line, and then plopping down a big foam beetle in little pockets of the slower water, trying to avoid the pampas grasses that guard it on both sides. Within a few casts, Rosenbauer lands an eighteen-inch brown, darkly colored, no doubt from spending its days hidden under the creek's cut banks. Just before he releases the fish, he turns it sideways. Its nose and tail pretty much reach the opposite banks.

Later in the day, we move on to the Ñirehuao, a proper spring creek that curves prettily through a valley. As we walk to the bank to take a closer look at the water, grasshoppers scatter in every direction. A few end up in the creek, and some of those disappear in the swirls of a rising trout.

After a quick lunch of rare roast beef and couscous, we begin to prowl the banks of the Ñirehuao, casting foam grasshopper imitations into likely holding spots. The fish we catch get bigger as the day progresses and warms, with the largest topping out at around twenty inches.

SECOND-CHANCE TROUT

Back at the lodge, the evening flows with wine and stories. The general sense is that the week had been perfectly weighted—a taste of the awe-inspiring rivers of Cinco Rios followed by the magical and intimate isolation of del Zorro.

The next morning—the last day for Hereford and me—we wake before sunrise for an early breakfast by the woodstove. Hereford, Rosenbauer, Galilea, Larsen, and I, along with Dan Dunn, a retired investor, and Jay Vinsel, a judge from Zanesville, Ohio, meet up with Galilea's cousin, Alejandro, a compact and dapper man who speaks very little English but has no trouble communicating his passion. We drive to the heights above the Valley of the Moon. Our mission is to find some Andean Condors, the largest flying bird on the planet, with wingspans that can reach almost eleven feet. We arrive at a spot above a nauseatingly high river canyon and wander in the biting wind until Alejandro spies a condor sitting on a cliffside nook. It is a juvenile—only one or two years old, Alejandro says—but it is enormous and magnificent nonetheless. We wait patiently as the sun emerges and warms the rocks of the cliff. The giant bird begins to pluck at its neck feathers, releasing them into the air as if testing the flying conditions. (One member of our party, who will remain nameless, begins to gather some of the neck feathers caught in the pampas grass for fly-tying material.)

The bird teases us some more, craning its neck, then stretching its wings before finally taking flight, a sight and scene that could be described, without hyperbole, as breathtaking. It immediately heads high in the sky, riding the thermals, with nary a flap of its wings. Other condors join in. Suddenly, as we watch, our bird comes toward us and does a flyby, which feels like, in anthropomorphic terms, a gesture of curiosity about this bundled-up gathering of bipeds who have been staring at it all morning.

That afternoon, for our last fishing session, Hereford and I head out with guide Sebastian Letelier to fish Zorro's home spring creek, which starts in Argentina and wends its way through the property, sheltering browns of up to twenty-six-inches in length. Letelier is forty-four and rake thin, with wild strands of hair that sprout from under his hat and a dark beard that trails down to his chest. He is a painter, a fly tier known the world over for his classic Atlantic salmon patterns, and a lover of bamboo rods, vintage Hardy reels, and beat-up oilcloth jackets. He guides with reverence for place and time and the quarry, moving slowly, weighing and considering each fly in his hand before tying it on. He has been through things, he says, and at one point years ago, burned out and exhausted, he nearly gave up painting, fly tying, and fishing, only to eventually recover and regain his footing.

"Eso . . . eso," he says, over and again, in barely more than a whisper as I cast, a Spanish word that, literally translated means "that," but is used by Letelier as an affirmation. It feels monastic in its repetition.

The fishing is technical, and we cast into small windows among the weed beds, through an unceasing twenty-mile-per-hour wind that ripples both the pampas grasses and Letelier's beard. Despite the weather, we catch fish, including two of the creek's giants landed by Hereford.

As the day nears its end, Letelier talks a bit about growing up fishing in Chile, and about how some of the rivers of his youth to the north are now mere shadows of their former selves thanks to dams, crowds, and a changing climate. He says that here, though, one can still bear witness to the almost unfathomable beauty of nature, in these unscathed landscapes and these pristine waters and their second-chance trout. Given the inevitability of human nature, it likely won't last forever. His advice? Get your ass down here.

2024

24

Fishing Through a Pandemic

It was a brisk and beautiful morning, the sky cloudless, the sunlight sharp. It was the kind of day that under different circumstances would have you looking forward to the coming seasons of warmth and splendor and carefree fun.

We began packing the car. I'll never forget the looks on some of my neighbors' faces as I took the bags of groceries—canned goods, pasta, rice, and yes, even some toilet paper—and crammed them in the back of the car. Those faces betrayed thoughts. *Wait, should I be doing the same thing?* Fear may be the only thing more contagious than this virus.

We left Brooklyn, home. We headed for Vermont. The emotions were mixed, uncomfortably.

There was relief. We would have more space, inside and out, in Vermont. We would be in a rural area, less friendly to contagion. Eighty percent of the intensive care unit beds in Brooklyn were already filled. Refrigerated trucks had been brought in for the bodies that didn't fit in the overwhelmed morgues. I had listened with growing anxiety as my city doctor friend had relayed the horror show in his hospital's ER the night before.

There was profound sadness: We were leaving our home, our city. When would we see it again? In two weeks? In two months? In a year or longer? What would we find when we returned? Surely, it would never be the same.

There was a stabbing sense of guilt: We were lucky enough to have somewhere else to go, a refuge, or at least something that approximated one. Those left behind would suffer. I felt like a chicken shit. I wouldn't be there to help if someone needed it. My neighbors. My city.

The news got grimmer as we traveled north. Testing still lagged, disastrously. The city, it had become apparent, was a hotspot. A lockdown was said to be coming. We were being told as a nation to pull together by staying apart.

At the last minute as my wife and I packed, just before I zipped my duffel bag, I'd thrown in a four-weight fly rod, a reel, and a box of flies. It was, at the time, merely a symbolic gesture. It was March. Most rivers in Vermont were closed. The fishing on the one open river would be poor if happening at all. The gear was a rather senseless thing to bring along, seeing as we required every inch we could get in the car. But I needed one totem of normalcy, a normalcy I now realized I had taken for granted all my life.

A week into the self-quarantine, we had some sort of routine in place. Our three little girls were doing their classes online under our supervision. We went for long, aimless walks, picking up sticks, talking about the dog we were going to get someday. We sat by the fire as a family in the evenings. We were together, which was its own sweet blessing.

I spent the days in quarantine as a teacher, a chef, the Minister of Fun, and head of an impromptu all-girl soccer academy. I worked in the margins, preparing for a book that was supposedly coming out in the fall, a piece of pre-plague writing that now felt quite naive. The days were immersive enough to take my mind off some of what was going on. But never all of it.

FISHING THROUGH A PANDEMIC

On a late afternoon of that first week, with temperatures in the fifties, I took a break from the routine and rigged up my fly rod. I walked the mile down to the river. The licking, burbling water coursing through the valley seemed to enhance, rather than engulf, all the other sounds around it, of the breeze in the creaking tree limbs, of the birdsong. As I walked the bank of the river, I passed many likely holding spots but did not make a cast. It felt reassuring to watch the water, to be reminded of its timelessness, to think of the girls making casts down here with me as the weather warmed. A swarm of midges hovered by the head of one slow pool. Little green shoots had begun to struggle their way up from the wet, squishy banks. The trees had gnarled bulbs on their branches, signs of the budding to come. "Spring is the earth forgiving itself," Allen Gurganus once wrote.

As I walked home, the sun began to ease itself behind the mountain in the distance. It grew cold and the breeze became more insistent. It was abundantly clear that we were in for difficult times, perhaps more difficult than we can even fathom, a cruel winter that would seem endless. I tried to prepare myself for the worst. But, I decided as I neared the house, I would also start living for the spring—whether actual or metaphorical—and for all those things I once took for granted. It may be months before we're there. It may take a year or longer. But it will come.

2020

25

Tier's Poker

Sid pushed two Elk-Hair Caddis into the pot, slowly—maybe even reluctantly—with what looked like worry furrowing his brow. Or was he bluffing? I was next and in a bit of a jam. In front of me on the old oak table was a fast-dwindling pile of feathers, dubbing, and barbed steel. I was not, as they say in Vegas, on a roll. I'd already lost six Pheasant Tail nymphs, two Light Hendricksons, and my prized green Double Bunny, a present from a Chilean friend. What remained was a conglomeration of frazzled cast-offs from the nether regions of my fly box, which bummed out my playing partners. They wanted any winnings to at least include something identifiable.

If I lost this one, I knew I was out. But I held a hand as colorful as a Royal Wulff—a full house, kings over jacks. I looked around the room, a tactic I'd seen good poker players use to suss out the competition. Charlie, who started the round of betting, was leaning back in his chair, tapping his foot to a Johnny Cash song on the radio while chewing the ice from his George Dickel on the rocks. His mottled heap of flies was three times the size of mine. Sid was still looking concerned, nervously flipping a Woolly Bugger in his hand, as if trying to let fate decide whether he should stay in the hand or not.

"All right," I said. "I'll see your Elk-Hair Caddis." I tossed in two flies that looked suspiciously like navel lint. Desperate times, desperate measures.

We were some two and a half hours from the city, near Hancock, New York, on the southwest flank of the Catskills, trying to squeeze one last drop from what had been a fine season on the Delaware and her branches. It was late October. The crowds that make this area the epicenter of the East Coast trout world had abandoned the rivers and bars and restaurants. The black trees that lined the ancient rolling hills stood austere and naked. We were the only guests at the Timberline Motel. The proprietor, an unfailingly cheerful German woman, seemed surprised to see anyone at all.

"I eez cold, no? I vill turn up zee heat for zee fishermen."

Like many, we'd been lured to the city by work. Charlie is an equity analyst, with a plan to work his way up the ladder just high enough to be able to move somewhere else. Sid is a doctor earning his chops as a resident in an inner-city emergency room, where he faces not only medical problems but language and cultural ones, as well. I am a fledgling writer, trying to find footing in a literate land of magazines, editors, and publishing houses.

Charlie, Sid, and I are also anglers. The city, as we discovered, is full of them, and they run the gamut from the legions of men—mostly poor immigrants—who cast bait into the East River hoping for a fat striper to bring home to the table to those with a touch of gray at the temples and a lilt to their speech that must come from the altitude of penthouse apartments who spend weeks, if not months, on private salmon water in Canada and aquamarine flats halfway around the world. Then there are those who fall somewhere in between, like Charlie, Sid, and me.

We, too, are subsistence anglers, though we do not fish for food. The trips we make to the Catskills throughout the spring, summer, and fall act as replenishment and a reminder that there is more to this world than

TIER'S POKER

one self-absorbed city, that there is something else out there. A lot of that something else, for us, involves the actual catching of fish, something we'd done with semi-regularity throughout the season.

But now, with a last call in the chill of late October, we were perhaps getting a bit greedy. And we were paying for it.

Every fishing trip has a defining moment that isolates it from all others. Maybe it's a languid evening spent fishing a hatch, or the hook pulling on a big fish that's forever lost to the depths, like an early morning dream. On this particular trip, it was five hours of miserable cold and unrelenting rain, numbed fingers and brains, and no fish. Not even one bite. And we still had a day to go. We'd left the river that day silent and defeated, wondering if the weekend would have been better spent in the city rather than ending the season on this sour, sniffling note.

But we made the best of it. Sid remembered the deck of cards he carried in his vest. Charlie remembered his sour mash whiskey. I remembered that these guys were damn good fly tiers.

After an early dinner, we rearranged the chairs in our room in the Timberline, broke out the Dickel, and laid out our fly boxes. It was determined that each player would choose ten flies from the other two, and that the rest of the "chips" were to be chosen from our own boxes. Charlie went straight for my Ed Shenk Sculpin, hand-tied by the Carlisle, Pennsylvania, master himself, a fly he'd had his eye on for a couple of years now. I should have hidden that one. But no matter. I knew where I could hurt him, too. Charlie's specialty is his carefully crafted bead-head Prince Nymphs in a size 12, with beautiful green thoraxes and perfect white wings. I chose three of them. And Sid had made a big deal about a new fly he'd recently tied, a black, orange, and purple streamer with rubber legs—the Trout Tamer, he'd named it. Ugly but effective, he claimed, like inguinal hernia repairs. (Whatever that meant—he was a doctor, remember.) Anyway, he'd been saving it for a special occasion. I chose that one, too.

"I'll see your March Browns," Charlie said, looking at the flies I had tossed into the pot. "I guess those were once March Browns."

Johnny Cash turned to Lucinda Williams on the radio, the clock struck midnight, and we knew we wouldn't push it tomorrow, that we'd be satisfied with the generous hand we'd been dealt this fishing season. It was time to lay our cards down for what was the biggest pot of the night—Leadwing Coachmans, caddis, nymphs of all kinds, Woolly Buggers, and even a few unrecognizables. Charlie had two pairs. Not bad. I laid down my full house. Sid's scowl turned into a smile. He showed his hand. Four of a kind. He'd been bluffing, indeed.

2000

26

Brookies Under Broadway

I recently came across a fun story written by National Public Radio's Robert Krulwich about Jack Gasnick, a hardware store owner in Manhattan who, in 1955, supposedly found fish flopping around the basement of his New York City store after it had been flooded by Hurricane Diane. Gasnick claimed the water came from a stream that ran under his building, 992 Second Avenue (at 53rd Street). Krulwich wrote that Gasnick even broke out a rod and reel and caught one of the fish in the flooded basement. It was a carp. And he ate it.

I'd heard another story like this, one told by the inimitable A. J. McClane, a redwood of twentieth-century fishing writing, which appears in one of his books, *McClane's Angling World*. It goes like this:

In 1956, when a water main broke on 58th street and Madison Avenue, plumbing expert Jack Gasnick found a brook trout flopping in the gutter as water poured down the street. Like most of his compatriots who worked the city underground, Mr. Gasnick had taken a variety of fish over the years including pickerel, carp, goldfish, smelt, catfish and eels. But this was his first trout, possibly a relic from the Turtle Bay Stream, which still meanders under the East 50s. According to Mr.

Gasnick, who has since netted trout in the flooded basements of 301 and 325 East 52nd street, the stream is audible, as it whimpers behind walls and below cellars.

McClane goes on to describe an instance in which a brook trout "erupted from the outlet pipe" of a building in Greenwich Village, which happened to be built over a stream known as Minetta Brook. (Minetta Lane, unlike its neighboring streets, meanders in S-curves, presumably just like the stream it was named for and built over.)

As a trout fisherman who is admittedly prone to bouts of nature nostalgia, I've always found McClane's anecdote irresistible. I'd never heard the carp version of the story until reading Krulwich's blog post.

But could any of this possibly be true? I decided to investigate by emailing John Waldman, a well-respected aquatic biologist at Queens College, for his take. He wasn't buying either story. Here's what Waldman wrote to me, about the brook trout in particular:

> My sense is the story is apocryphal. If not, then these fish got in through the water supply system. But I'd go with it just never happened. The idea that generations of brook trout lived in the dark in a presumably nearly foodless ecosystem is nonsensical. I find that urbanites are prone to romanticizing wildness foregone.

Guilty as charged! But the stories jibed with me for this reason: I've always had this sense that New York City, and perhaps the island of Manhattan most of all, was once some sort of near-Edenic paradise, long lost now of course. This idea was encouraged by Eric W. Sanderson's book, *Mannahatta: A Natural History of New York City*, which attempted to re-create what the island of Manhattan looked like, ecologically speaking, in 1609 when the explorer Henry Hudson first saw it.

My theory about New York City has something to do with its fundamental essence, so long gone and so deeply repressed that it's likely now found only in our gene memory. Here's my belief, backed up (somewhat) by Sanderson's book: New York was once one of the most naturally bountiful and beautiful places in this country. That was the initial attractor, which led, inexorably, to the many millions of humans who inhabit it now. The city was a victim, and not a beneficiary, of its geography, as the journalist Raymond Moley had once written. One of my best friends, a John Muir–worshipping Californian, thinks I'm full of crap, that this theory of mine is just another example of a typical a-hole New Yorker's hubris and self-absorption. He may be right. But stay with me a minute here.

When Europeans first came to what is now New York, hunting unsuccessfully for a route to China, they found a twelve-mile-long island that the Natives, the Lenapes, called Mannahatta, which means "the land of many hills." Sluicing through that hilly land were numerous freshwater spring creeks, like Minetta Brook and the ones that still run under the East 50s. Deer and elk roamed in what is now Times Square. Turkeys strutted on Wall Street (some say they still do . . . *ba dum tsh*). The weather was temperate and the land was protected from storms by what would later be named Long Island. To the east was a tidal strait (the misnamed East River) teeming with striped bass, blackfish, and fluke that came in with each replenishing tide. To the west was the mouth of a fertile river (the Hudson) packed with oysters, more stripers, sturgeon, shad, porgies, and bluefish. The Lenapes had huge fishing camps in the sections of the city now known as Harlem and the Bronx.

So, paradise was paved. But we didn't stop with the parking lot.

When I walk around the city or fish its (still) great surrounding saltwater, I often think of those last few elegiac paragraphs of *The Great Gatsby*, in which Fitzgerald describes the Dutch sailors first laying eyes on the area that's a little ways to the east of Manhattan, that "fresh, green breast of the new world," and that "transitory enchanted moment" when

> man must have held his breath in the presence of this conti-
> nent, compelled into an aesthetic contemplation he neither

understood nor desired, face to face for the last time in history with something commensurate to his capacity for wonder.

I can't help but think that somehow—perhaps also within our gene memory or maybe just when we stroll the serpentine Minetta Lane—we *feel* those lost streams bubbling underneath us with their (possible) brook trout, and hold on to just a touch of that capacity for wonder.

2011

27

The Beast

The story begins in the first week of March on Dixon Lake in Escondido, California, a reservoir full of clear Colorado River water, there to slake the thirst of San Diego's suburbs. Dixon seems incapable of doing anything more significant than that. All told, it's only seventy featureless acres. In a rented Valco aluminum boat powered by a trolling motor, you can go from one end to the other in under ten minutes. But size isn't everything.

Or is it?

An old man, a lake regular whom everyone calls Six Pack, mans his usual post on what's known as the handicap dock at Dixon. It's morning, and the fog has just begun to burn off the hills. The old man holds a light spinning rod rigged with two-pound-test. On the point of a small hook he's stuck a BB-size ball of Power Bait. He's fishing for trout, and Dixon is a good place to do that. Some thirty thousand pounds of rainbow trout are planted in the tiny lake each year, courtesy of the California Department of Fish and Game. Fishermen aren't the only beneficiaries. "Nobody feeds their bass as well as we do," says lake ranger Jim Dayberry.

150   RIVERS ALWAYS REACH THE SEA

The old man already has a few good trout on his stringer when his bobber starts to dance again. He lifts his rod and sets the hook, gently, because of the light line. He reels, feeling a rhythmic pulse. He lets his mind wander a bit, thinking ahead to the trout fillets he'll eat that night.

But just as he has it nearly in, the hooked trout goes berserk, zigging and zagging in wild figure eights. There's an explosion of water, and the light tug of the trout is suddenly gone, replaced by a brutish grab that seems to want to pull him, the dock, and the sky in with it. He spots his trout in the maw of something impossibly large. In a second, the pull is gone. The old man is left with his frayed line coiled like a pig's tail, his rod lifeless, his mouth agape. Later that morning, Six Pack stutters as he tries to recount the tale to a dock attendant. No one believes him. And no one realizes it at the time, but the old man had just hooked the biggest bass in the world.

Nearly two weeks later, on March 19, a cool Sunday morning, Jed Dickerson, thirty-three, and Kyle Malmstrom, thirty-four, are in line at the concession stand at Dixon Lake waiting to get their permits. Dickerson is at the very front, Malmstrom just a step behind. They each fork over $30, then hustle down to the dock to the rented boats, the only type allowed. They race to attach the trolling motors they'd brought along. Malmstrom is the first one off. He heads north. Dickerson glances over at the handicap dock. It's one of his go-to spots, but three trout anglers are fishing from the shore nearby. He decides not to bother them and heads east.

For the past five years, Dickerson, along with his two best friends, Mac Weakley, thirty-three, and Mike "Buddha" Winn, thirty-two, have been chasing the next world-record largemouth bass. Their dedication to this pursuit has hurtled from pastime into obsession. Working flexible nighttime hours in the casino industry has allowed them to fish nearly eight hundred days among the three of them in those five years, on Dixon and a handful of other San Diego reservoirs that are the epicenter of the

THE BEAST

151

hunt for the world-record bass. Their persistence has reaped rewards. In 2003, Weakley caught a nineteen-pound eight-ounce bass from Dixon, good enough for twelfth place on the list of the top twenty-five biggest largemouths ever recorded. Later that same year, Dickerson landed the fourth-largest bass of all time, a twenty-one-pound eleven-ounce monster, also from Dixon. The trio is well-known for their dedication and skill. Dickerson has always been the most fervent of the three, the one for whom the quest has taken on its own life. He's out here early on this Sunday morning as Weakley and Winn sleep in.

Malmstrom is also a record hunter, though his obsession is limited by his nine-to-five job as an estate-planning consultant. But he has caught some notable bass, including one close to fifteen pounds. He speaks in a laid-back drawl and spends most of his free time at Dixon. "You always get that magical feeling going up there that any day could be *the* day," he says.

On this morning, he drives his boat backward, led by his trolling motor. It's the preferred style of Dixon's big-bass hunters, providing precise control and clear sight lines into the water. He works the shoreline, peering into the depths, searching for the cleared-off rings that indicate a bass bed.

He comes around to the handicap dock. The spot is now empty. Just as Malmstrom nears the dock, he sees a massive shadow shoot from the shallows under his boat into the deep water. "My first thought was 'Holy crap, that's an eighteen-plus,'" he says. He anchors on the shore, waits for fifteen minutes, then idles over to see if she's returned. He spots her, maybe ten feet away, slowly inching back to the nest. "Then I decide to wait her out," Malmstrom says. For two hours he sits, far enough away not to spook her again but close enough to guard his spot from other anglers, especially Dickerson.

At nine A.M., he can't wait any longer and motors over. He sees the bass hovering above her nest and feels a shot of adrenaline. Tying the front of his boat to the dock, he drops an anchor off the back. The day has cleared and there's no wind on the water: perfect sight-fishing conditions. Malmstrom casts for the fish, throwing jigs and swimbaits, teasing the lures across the nest, trying to agitate her into striking.

After two hours of fruitless casting, he's tense and excited and can no longer keep his find to himself. He does something he will later regret: he calls Dickerson on his cellphone. The two men, though they compete for the same fish, have a cordial relationship. "I'm on a big one," he boasts. Dickerson, who's on the other side of the lake, immediately relays that information to Weakley and Winn, who are now awake.

Weakley and Winn show up at the handicap dock at one P.M. Dickerson joins them and they watch Malmstrom throw casts over the enormous bass. A local teenager, Dan Barnett, his interest piqued by the commotion, joins the party of onlookers. Malmstrom knows this is a special bass and decides he will fish for her all day if he has to. But he has a problem—he needs to call his wife to tell her he won't be home anytime soon, and his cellphone has just died. He asks Weakley if he can borrow his. They work out a trade: Weakley will let him use his phone if Malmstrom will show him the fish. Malmstrom makes his call, then Weakley jumps in the boat and gets his first good look at the bass. "My God," he says, "that's Jed's fish," recognizing it as the twenty-one-pound eleven-ounce bass Dickerson had caught three years earlier.

Back on the dock, Weakley, lusting after what he knows is at least a twenty-pounder, begins pestering Malmstrom. "Come on, give me a shot. I guarantee you I can catch it." Malmstrom refuses. Weakley offers him $1,000 for thirty minutes on the fish, showing a roll of $100 bills to Barnett on the dock. Malmstrom refuses again. "I wouldn't have been able to live with myself," he says, "if Mac caught that fish."

He stays until dark but leaves the lake empty-handed. The big bass might have hit his jig once, he thinks, but he isn't sure. He's bone-tired. He contemplates calling in sick the next day to come back for the fish, but then, feeling a twinge of guilt, decides against it.

Just before the concession stand closes, Winn buys a camping permit, which allows access to the grounds, but not the lake, before the outside gates open at six A.M. The trio is determined to be first on this fish the

THE BEAST   153

next day. But they'll have competition: Dan Barnett, fourteen, calls his eighteen-year-old brother, Steve, and they decide to come out to Dixon early the next morning to take their shot.

In retrospect, Malmstrom says he learned two things that day. "I'm never calling those meatheads ever again when I'm on a big fish," he says with a chuckle. "And I'll be sure to take the next day off from work."

⚬━━⚬

Weakley, Dickerson, and Winn grew up in Escondido. They met in the fourth grade and have been best friends ever since, bonds forged by the anguish of broken families. In a span of two years when they were teenagers, Weakley's father died of a heart attack and both Dickerson's and Winn's parents split up. The boys escaped by spending hours trout fishing on nearby Dixon Lake.

In his twenties, Weakley began to frequent the Native American casinos that had popped up in the area, becoming a regular at the low-stakes poker tables. One day a man approached him, impressed by the clean-cut young man's knowledge of, and hunger for, gambling. He offered Weakley a job as a manager in his company, Pacific Gaming, which provides the betting cash for casinos in Southern California. Weakley liked the job, liked hanging out at casinos and card rooms, liked the high-risk vibe and the big money. He was good at watching the cash and his boss told him to hire two lieutenants. Weakley hired Dickerson, who had been installing carpets, and Winn, who had been working as a first mate on a deep-sea fishing boat. The trio hung out together every day on the job and off, when they trout fished on Dixon Lake.

At the beginning of 2001, they noticed that Mike Long, who was then the unquestioned king of the San Diego big-bass scene—still years away from his dramatic fall from grace due to allegations of cheating in tournaments—was fishing Dixon nearly every day. He seemed to be onto something, working his boat slowly along the shoreline, staring into the water, as if the lake's bottom were lined with gold. In a sense it was: that year, an outfit in Tampa called the Big Bass Record Club was offering

$8 million to the angler who broke George Washington Perry's iconic 1932 world record for largemouth bass. The three friends, ever the gamblers, liked the odds of finding that fish in their home lake, which they knew so well. They ditched their trout gear, bought heavier rods, and became bass fishermen.

Their methods were primitive at first. Plastic worms and live shiners were their bait, not the jigs and swimbaits serious big-bass hunters preferred. Determined to learn, they approached Mike Long to pick his brain, but he spurned the upstarts. So they studied him on the water from afar and found out how to fish for big bass the hard way. That year, the trio logged more than two hundred days at Dixon.

In the spring of 2001, they were bystanders as Mike Long caught a twenty-pound twelve-ounce bass from Dixon, the eighth largest ever at the time, and the first recorded over twenty pounds in a decade. That only made the trio fish harder, even as the Big Bass Record Club, along with its $8 million bounty, disappeared. Why they fished now wasn't because of money but something else entirely: they had become too good to stop.

In 2003, Weakley caught a 17-8, then the 19-8. Later that spring, Dickerson capped it all with the 21-11, the fish that officially put the men on the big-bass map. Long was at the lake on the day Dickerson landed that fish and claimed that it was the same one he had caught two years earlier, when it was a pound lighter. The evidence: it had the same dime-size black dot underneath its jaw. A few weeks later, Long said some trout-fishing friends had found the fish floating dead; he'd sent the carcass to a taxidermist. Weakley never believed him. "Total b.s.," he says. He suspected Long was just trying to keep the hordes off his honeyhole, figuring someone could catch that fish again, and this time it just might be the actual world record.

Mike Long had good reason to worry.

○══○

At four A.M. on March 20, Jed Dickerson flashes his camping permit and passes through the gates at Dixon. Weakley and Winn are getting

THE BEAST   155

doughnuts and coffee. The night before, the trio hatched their plan. Underlying their conversations was something they didn't dare verbalize: *This bass could be the one.*

Weakley and Winn arrive at five A.M. The three of them gather in Weakley's car and listen to the radio. Dazed by the early morning hour, they barely utter a word until Weakley, pointing at the windblown streaks of rain on the car window, says, "Man, what the hell are we doing here?" They laugh, knowing the answer.

Meanwhile, Dan and Steve Barnett nudge their car up to the Dixon gate outside the grounds, but at six A.M., after running to the concession stand to get their permits, they glance down to the water and see Weakley, Winn, and Dickerson already in a boat. The camping permit has worked. The Barnett brothers, with no shot at the fish, opt to watch the action from the handicap dock. Chris Bozir, a part-time dock attendant, joins them.

Winn, as always, mans the motor. Weakley and Dickerson stand, rods ready. They ease toward the handicap dock. Wind and rain make it impossible to see anything more than the shadow of the fish. But she's there.

The first cast is Dickerson's. Tossing out his white Bob Sangster jig underhand, he lets it sink to the bottom and sit, a foot or two away from the fish. Then he works the lure over the nest. He jerks the rod tip, making the skirt billow and contract. The bass turns but doesn't take. Weakley then tosses in his jig. The huge female's consort, a three-pound male, gets agitated, racing around the bed and diving on the lure.

Dickerson and Weakley continue to alternate casts. Three times, Dickerson thinks the bass bumps his lure, and he instinctively swings his rod but fails to connect. The visibility is so poor that he can't be sure if it's the male or the female hitting his jig. Weakley tries to set the hook a few times, and also comes up empty. No one—either on the boat or the dock—is talking much.

After forty-five minutes, Weakley feels his line twitch again, and he swings hard. This time, his rod doubles in half. Time doesn't slow down as it's supposed to. It speeds up. The fish dives for deeper water, jerking the fifteen-pound-test line from his reel. She begins to give in a bit and he reels, fast. Weakley knows truly big bass don't fight that well. Their obscene girth tires them quickly, like a four-hundred-pound man trying to climb stairs.

When Weakley gets the bass close to the boat, Winn reaches down with the net but misses. With new life, the bass runs hard for the handicap dock and the audience gathered there. Weakley pulls on his rod with all his strength, determined to keep her away from the dock's pilings. He turns her head, then easily reels her in. This time, Winn gets her with one scoop.

To the Barnett brothers, this is the most exciting thing they have ever witnessed on the water. The scene has played out not fifteen feet away, and now the show has reached its climax. "That's an insanely enormous bass," Steve remarks.

But then he sees something else, something that deflates his euphoria. The white jig is embedded in the fish's back, maybe three inches behind the dorsal fin. Steve groans and yells, "Oh man, it's foul-hooked!" Weakley and Winn glance in the direction of the yell, momentarily distracted from the black-and-silver mass of fish in the net.

Their attention quickly returns to the bass. Winn unhooks the jig and runs a stringer through the fish's mouth. Though the fight took little physical energy, the three men are breathing heavily. Lying on the boat's bottom is the biggest bass any of these men have ever seen. It's the one.

They should feel total elation, but Weakley keeps looking down at a spot on the fish's back, the hole left by the jig. *I foul-hooked the damn thing*, he thinks. Then he hears voices on the dock. The audience is clamoring to see the fish up close. Winn hears them, too. Reaching for the trolling motor, he instead heads for the middle of the lake after his friends lower the stringer into the water. The trio talk for a few minutes, casting occasional glances at the fish tied to the boat. They lift her out of the water and put her on Dickerson's handheld Berkley scale: 25.5. The weight is far above the magical mark of twenty-two pounds four ounces. They motor back to the dock.

THE BEAST   157

The moments there are chaotic and quick. They hang the fish on the scale again. Now it shows 25.1 pounds. Weakley gets out his video camera and shoots the footage of the fish that will later appear on ESPN and various evening news shows. Toward the end of the shaky clip, the camera pans in on the fish, and a disembodied voice from somewhere behind it utters five words: "That's the beast right there."

Dickerson wants to take a photo of Weakley with the fish, but Weakley says his arm is too tired from lifting it. Winn stands in, grabbing the fish with one arm. The photo is snapped. Later that day, it would fly around the Internet, incorrectly captioned as "Mac Weakley."

Weakley and Dickerson look at the fish more closely. They notice something: a dime-size black dot under the fish's jaw. "I'm one hundred percent sure that this is the same fish I caught in 2003," says Dickerson, which, of course, would make it the same fish that Mike Long caught in 2001. A replica mount from the 2003 catch was featured on the cover of *Field & Stream*. This is a bass accustomed to the limelight. Then the men notice something else: a short strand of two-pound-test running out of the bass's mouth. Remember Six Pack, the old trout fisherman?

Then Steve Barnett hears either Weakley or Dickerson say, "Look, there's a mark on its back." He can't quite remember who uttered those words amid all the excitement. Steve is confused, not exactly sure what the comment means, what whoever said it is trying to imply. "We saw you foul-hook it, though," Steve says, pleading almost, still unsure. Then he hears Weakley tell Winn to release the fish. Winn unhooks the stringer, and the biggest bass in the world swims lazily away and disappears.

The beast? Well, that turns out to be something else entirely.

A ranger at Dixon makes a phone call to a friend, the first trickle of what will become a flood. It builds with more phone calls, then emails and Internet chat-room postings. Within a few hours, the first news stories hit the wires.

At first the attention is fun for the men. This is the fish they have worked so hard for, justification for the hours, days, months, and years they've been after it. "You always heard people claiming that they saw a twenty-five-pounder," says Weakley. "We proved it exists."

Over the next two days, Weakley does dozens of interviews—the *New York Times*, *Los Angeles Times*, the Associated Press, *The Early Show* on CBS. ESPN sends a camera crew to the lake. They retest Dickerson's scale with a five-pound weight. It's perfectly accurate. News reports deem the fish the new world record, even as they note the ambiguous manner in which the fish was caught and documented. An IGFA official is quoted as saying the foul hooking may or may not matter, and that Weakley should submit his application anyway. The one sticking point seems to be a California state regulation that says any fish not caught in the mouth must be released immediately.

In the beginning, Weakley contemplates going against his own first impulse and sending in the photo, the videos, and the testimony of the five witnesses to the IGFA. He's buoyed by the praise, caught up in the attention.

But quickly, the murmurs of a conspiracy become shouts. People start to focus on the negative: There's the foul hooking. The fact that the fish wasn't weighed on a certified scale, even though there was one maybe one hundred feet away in the ranger's office. The lack of measurements of the fish's length and girth. "These boys know the rules better than anyone and they didn't follow them," says Ray Scott, the founder of B.A.S.S. and a voice to be reckoned with because of his considerable influence on the IGFA record committee.

For some, the questions become broader. What are the ethics of fishing for a spawning bass on its bed? What about the unnaturalness of California bass, Florida transplants that are basically hand-fed thousands of pounds of planted rainbow trout? The attacks even get personal. These guys work in the shadowy world of gambling. What about the unsavory nature of the $1,000 offer and the camping permit?

Less than forty-eight hours after catching his fish, Weakley sits in his house, hollow-eyed, exhausted. Winn has been on the internet, checking

THE BEAST

the pulse of the bass-fishing nation. After agonizing over the question with Winn and Dickerson, Weakley decides he doesn't want to prolong the negativity. He goes with his initial gut instinct. He foul-hooked the fish. It shouldn't count. He won't pursue the record.

"I know we did the right thing," says Weakley. "Look, we got to hold a twenty-five-pound bass. No one else ever has. That was cool for us." He thinks it's all over now, but the calls still stream in at all hours of the day and night. Local newspaper writers approach him with proposals for screenplays. Eventually, he's overwhelmed and turns off his phone, done with the telling and retelling.

Meanwhile on Dixon, there's world-record hysteria. Lake ranger Jim Dayberry estimates business is up 80 percent over normal. On many days, some thirty boats jockey for space on the tiny body of water. "And everyone coming in here says they want a shot at that bass," Dayberry says. A man flies in from Texas and rents a motor home and fishes for a week. Anglers from at least twenty different states have called asking about reservations. Amidst it all, an old man sits at his normal post, fishing for trout.

The irony, of course, is that George Washington Perry's fish, the twenty-two-pound four-ouncer caught in the backwoods of Georgia in 1932, would have been just as controversial, if not more so, in our modern age. There's no authenticated photo of his fish and no mount. Nobody ever made contact with the only witness to the catch. Perry simply weighed his fish at a country store and sent the information to a *Field & Stream* contest. Then he took the bass home and ate it.

But Perry's story, true or not, carries incredible resonance to this day. It's a symbol of a more innocent age, of the egalitarian American ideal that any man, no matter his station in life, can achieve greatness. It's grown more powerful over the years, snowballing in the way stories passed down from generation to generation tend to do. It's no coincidence that it's primarily older men who are Perry's fiercest protectors. This new era of nakedly ambitious record chasing seems to them to be blasphemous, a perversion of the right way—and the right reasons—to fish.

Months after Weakley caught his fish, the media firestorm has burned down to smoldering embers, now almost gone. As he sits in his house in Carlsbad, his eight-month-old boy asleep in the next room, Weakley is finally able to reflect. What he finds isn't that pretty. "I look back now and it all seems kind of sick," he says. "Fishing is supposed to be fun." Maybe like it was when he was a teenager and he and Winn and Dickerson would head to Dixon to blow off steam and fish for trout. He thinks about some of the stories that were written, of the excessive importance given to this record, the opinions, the controversy, the personal attacks—the real beast that emerged from the water that day.

"I see how stupid it all is. It's actually been a nice wake-up call," he says. "Me and Buddha and Jed realize now that we should get out and live life and spend more time with our families rather than being obsessed with a fish. It's just a fish. Just a stupid fish."

But that fish may be back next spring, drawn into Dixon's shallows by the urge to spawn. And, more likely than not, Weakley, Dickerson, and Winn will be there too, lured by another, equally powerful urge.

2006

28

Toots

I was ten years old the first time I ever saw a gun actually pointed at someone. I was in a little green johnboat on our family's bass lake in Alabama, perched in the bow. I held a short cane fly rod across my knees. My mother was lounging in the middle seat, drinking a Coke from a sweat-beaded glass, sunning her legs. She never cared much for fishing or this lake, but she was happy to be toted about in the boat like some Alabama Cleopatra.

My grandfather, whom we called Toots, was manning the small trolling motor in the back, telling off-color jokes that made me laugh and my mother wince. It was October, warm, the fool's summer, as Toots called it. Even as a ten-year-old, I felt the sweet sadness of days like this, of trying to appreciate something with the full knowledge of its impending departure.

We rounded a bend. There, on a grassy knoll, lay a man on his back, arms behind his head, legs crossed, with one foot dangling in the air. He was wearing tight jeans. He had a black mustache and held a long, white cigarette in his teeth. He looked contemplative, leisurely, like Walton's Piscator on the banks of the Lea.

"Get the fuck off my property!" Toots yelled. The man merely arched an eyebrow at us, as if we were apparitions from a daydream.

"*Daddy*," my mother hissed, nodding my way.

162   RIVERS ALWAYS REACH THE SEA

The man didn't move. Toots reached down, fumbling with something hidden near the trolling motor. He then stood up, rocking the boat, and pointed a small black handgun at the man. I'd never seen it before. The man didn't need another hint. He scampered into the woods like a spooked deer, leaving behind his half-smoked cigarette, which lay smoldering the grass.

In the late 1950s, Toots bought some land twenty miles northeast of his home in Birmingham, Alabama. It was just far enough from town to be properly called the sticks. Out of a marshy convergence of two streams on the property, he dug what he quite grandly called "Lake Tadpole," even though the body of water was really just five acres or so in size. Toots always liked to dress up the otherwise pedestrian. It was part of his steadfast belief that one must throw oneself, heart and soul, into any endeavor.

For two long decades, his primary endeavor was red whiskey. Toots was a secretive and volatile drunk, ravenously fumbling for the thick glass bottle hidden in the pantry as he loosened his work tie before dinner. His neglect of everything but his booze during those years made life hell for my grandmother, my uncle, and my mother.

On his fifty-fifth birthday, Toots quit drinking cold turkey and turned that voluminous energy toward the more benign but no less consuming addiction of fly-fishing. That was the Toots I knew.

Sometime in the 1970s Toots built a small cabin on Lake Tadpole. It was literally right on the shore, so when you looked out of the kitchen windows, it seemed like you were actually in the water, on a houseboat. It was a man's cabin, grander in the mind than in the physical particulars. The eat-in kitchen had yellow linoleum floors and a fridge with one of those water pump-like metal handles. The living room was furnished with a wooden rocking chair, a dusty brown couch, and a rabbit-eared black-and-white TV so Toots could watch the Bear—an old drinking pal—coach the Crimson Tide. The cabin's roof was tin. When it rained, it sounded like fingers drumming.

TOOTS 163

The cabin was musty and dark and stayed relatively cool without air conditioning even on a blazing Alabama August day. Toots always had the fridge filled with pull-tab cans of Coke. He let me drink as many as I wanted. In the doorjamb there was usually a crumbling wasp's nest. For a few years a big lazy water moccasin lived under the front stairs.

My favorite part of the cabin, though, was the covered boathouse connected to it through a door in the kitchen. It had two slips for Toots's green johnboats. Pond water gently lapped against the hulls with even the slightest hint of wind. On the boathouse walls Toots hung his five flyrods, all of them cane. The rods had some sort of kinetic aura to them, the promise of potentiality.

Neither my mother nor my grandmother ever really took to Tadpole, mostly because of the neighbors with their missing teeth and those distant sounds of chainsaws and echoes of shotgun reports. Toots, to his debit, never took the time to get to know them. And they never took too kindly to the incursion of a city slicker. They shattered his windows with rocks and stole his fridge full of Cokes.

But Toots only saw this as a minor price to pay for the joy he found at Tadpole. His deep-chested laugh—which boomed across Tadpole like its own shotgun blast—came easy there. He would sit in the back of the boat, one big paw on the quiet trolling motor, the other on his cane rod. He was never much of a false-caster, preferring to keep his fly in the water as much as possible. He was a patient teacher. As I slapped the water on both sides of the boat, he never scolded, only encouraged. He made a quarter-pound bream seem like a thousand-pound marlin. He told me about Montana, Iceland, Islamorada, and all the finned creatures that lived in those places. His grandkids—my two younger brothers and me and my uncle's three kids—represented his second chance.

At Tadpole I learned how to fly-fish on eager bream that sucked in small poppers with an audible *smooch*. I eventually moved up a few popper sizes and started catching largemouth bass. I loved that lake, loved that spooky cabin with all of its cobwebs and mustiness. I wanted to live there with Toots when I grew up.

My father got a job in North Carolina when I was eleven and we moved away. I eventually went off to school, bringing with me the Orvis impregnated bamboo eight-for-a-six Toots had given me, using the lessons he had taught me at Tadpole on northeastern trout streams. I didn't see Toots or Tadpole much during those years. I was too far away and too busy and absorbed with my own life—little boy blue and the man in the moon and all that—to think of much else. I lost touch with that ten-year-old, that sense of the fool's summer, of appreciating something before it's gone for good.

○━━○

Toots never stopped going to Tadpole. Not until he became ill, the effects of his drinking finally taking its toll on his liver.

He made one final trip to his lake in 1989. On one of those Alabama spring evenings that feel as soft as cashmere, Toots snuck out of the redbrick house in the tony suburb of Birmingham and stole away in the big dark blue Buick that had been gathering dust in the garage. My grandmother was playing bridge in town. Toots wasn't supposed to be driving; he was a menace to the local mailbox population.

He got to Tadpole in twenty-five minutes. By this time his cabin had been neglected for years. The screen door hung ajar. The exterior had become a backstop for the neighbors' target practice. The TV and fridge had been lifted long ago. Toots didn't even take a look inside.

He took his rod from the car. It still had a yellow popper tied to it from God knows how long ago. He stood on what was left of the boathouse dock and took a cast and jerked the popper back to the shore. He cast again and let the popper sit, the lake water around it rippling in growing concentric circles. An enormous bass engulfed the fly, dove for the bottom, and snapped the line. Toots returned to his car and left Tadpole immediately. Three weeks later, in a hospital room in Birmingham, his liver would fail for good.

I returned to Tadpole a few months after Toots died. I was still a teenager, years away from manhood. The water and surrounding trees looked as beautiful as ever. The cabin had been burned completely to the ground by then. It felt right in some strange way, like the embers of a funeral pyre or a physical manifestation of that form of unexpressed love we call grief. I thought of the joy contained here in this place. I thought of that laugh, booming across the water.

2016

29

Retrieved

The beginning of the end comes one sultry night in Key West. An evening like so many here, Nathaniel Linville thinks, even as he wonders if he'll be around to ever witness another. Linville has just used the last of his cocaine. It's only a temporary fix, though, something to stave off the crushing, terrifying pain of withdrawal from his other addiction, heroin.

He walks out of his apartment—its floor covered with newspapers, a month's worth of dirty clothes, and scattered piles of needles—into the darkened streets. He has a hundred dollars in his pocket, what's left of his money. He owes far more than that amount to every dealer in town, so this is a fishing expedition, and a blind one at that.

In the shadows, just off a backstreet, he spots a man sitting on a piece of old coral rock, exactly the type of man, Linville knows after all these years, that he's looking for. He sits down next to him. The man pulls out a crack pipe, takes a hit, then offers it to Linville. Linville inhales a hit and wipes his dripping nose—a telltale sign the dope sickness is already beginning—and tells the man he is looking for that "boy," slang for the heroin he so desperately wants.

"I got you," the man says. "I *got* you."

Linville hands him all his money. He knows better, but the cocaine and the fear and the sickness override any logic. The man walks away, swearing he'll be right back. *Just wait right here.* Linville does as he's told. The hours tick away. He eventually returns to his apartment, empty-handed, and sits on the edge of his bed. He is totally broke, out of drugs, and shaking with the sickness. He decides at that moment, he needs help.

It's eleven years later, the winter of 2021. Nathaniel Linville is standing in the bow of a skiff floating on a turtle grass flat near Man Key, just off Key West. He is tall and dark-haired, with maybe a week's worth of scruff on his face, and stout from the weightlifting he does religiously.

The water ripples as it hurries off the flat with the falling tide. Linville scans the area, looking for any disturbance in the matrix of brown and green grasses, white spots of sand, and turquoise-stained deeper holes—a mud, a mooning flash of silver, a tail—any sign of the maddening and obsessed-over fish known as a permit.

On the platform on the back of the skiff, scrutinizing the flat from his higher perch, stands John O'Hearn. He is a forty-eight-year-old native Baltimorean who has been guiding in Key West for twenty-two years. He has carvings of permit on his belt buckle and necklace.

Linville and O'Hearn have fly-fished for permit together for nearly four hundred days over the past dozen years. Of the astounding 254 permit Linville has caught in his life, around half have been with O'Hearn, including a sixteen-pounder that is the standing world record for the fish on two-pound tippet. In recent years, they have won three permit tournaments, which rank among the most competitive fishing competitions in the world. Today, they are "trying to solve another problem that has never been solved before," as Linville describes it. That is, they are attempting to catch a permit of over twenty-four pounds with four-pound tippet, *the* fish that would break a world record which has stood for thirty years. Success would bring Linville's fly rod world record count to five: along with the two-pound tippet permit record, he also has the six-pound record for tarpon and the two- and four-pound records for whaler sharks.

RETRIEVED 169

Linville, who is thirty-nine, is clean and sober. He owns a business (The Angling Company, a Key West fly shop), and is a husband and new father. He is intense, articulate, and assertive in his beliefs. He is also, as the fly-fishing icon Andy Mill has described him, "probably the best saltwater fly angler in the world right now."

"I see something," O'Hearn says.

"Donde?" Linville asks.

"I had a tail to the left there, about eighty feet."

"That darker section out there?"

"Yeah, right in front of it."

Linville stares, craning his neck forward and standing like a fencer, one arm behind his back, the other pointing his rod.

"That's where he is," O'Hearn says.

A moment later, the permit shows itself, its scimitar-like tail popping up, slashing the air, as if accepting a duel that's tipped decidedly in its favor. The fish doesn't look quite big enough for the record, but there's only one way to know for sure.

Linville begins his cast. Unlike many flats fishermen, he is not rushed or overcome with anxiety when he spots a fish. His casting stroke is long, graceful, and, most notably, slow. "Nat is unquestionably the best caster I've ever seen," O'Hearn says. It is a remarkable thing to witness, this illusion those at the top of a sport can create—think Michael Jordan in midair—of slowing down time.

After two false casts, Linville lays down the fly maybe two feet to the left of the fish, so the current will swing it in to it. He makes a series of long, slow strips. The fish swoops over for a look at the fly . . . then zips away, off the flat, ending a fairly typical encounter.

"I maybe could have led him a bit more?" Linville says.

"Maybe," O'Hearn says. "But I think you did everything right."

Permit possess neither the sleek shape of a bonefish nor the beautiful brawn of a tarpon. They look like oversize pompano; both fish are members of the jack family. They live primarily in the western Atlantic's deep water, from Massachusetts down to the eastern coast of South America (they have closely related family members in both the Pacific and Indian Oceans). But in certain parts of the world, they come shallow, cruising the flats in search of food, like crabs and shrimp. It is on those flats where true permit fanatics come into contact with them. And there is no place more hallowed for chasing permit on the flats than the Florida Keys.

As the sport of flats fishing for bonefish and tarpon began to ascend in the 1960s and '70s, permit were mostly an afterthought, regarded as no more worth a cast than the barracuda or jacks that also sometimes come shallow. Even when some anglers began to target them, they remained a back-burner fish, primarily because of their difficulty. They can be—in the Keys, especially—an exasperating fish, hard to find and harder to fool. Weeks and even months can go by without catching one, or even really having a good shot. Even the best permit guides, like O'Hearn—who fishes for them maybe sixty days a year—catch very few, maybe twenty-five a year. The most famous story ever written about the species (Thomas McGuane's "The Longest Silence") is about all of the time you spend *not* catching them. The famous flats fishing guide Steve Huff describes permit as "dishonest" fish. "You can do everything exactly right," he says, meaning the cast, and the placement and movement of the fly, "and they will still screw you."

Despite his sentiment, it is Huff and the angler Del Brown who are widely credited with popularizing fly-fishing for permit in the 1980s.

Other anglers had, of course, fished for them well before then, but it was the duo's single-minded pursuit of the fish—and the proof that the nervous Nellies could, indeed, actually be caught with relative frequency—that caused their esteem to soar.

During his fishing career, Brown, who is considered the GOAT of the discipline, caught 513 permit (the vast majority of them with Huff) with a fly rod and once held seven world records for them (all but one with Huff). Two of those records still stand, nineteen years after his death, one of them the four-pound record Linville is attempting to break. The other is the biggest fly rod permit ever recorded by the International Game Fish Association (IGFA)—the keeper of fishing world records—a forty-one-pound, eight-ounce giant caught near Key West on a flat that has since been known as Scene of the Crime.

Permit are deeply polarizing fish. One is either madly obsessed with them or wholly put off by them. Linville and O'Hearn stand firmly within the former camp. The difficulty, they believe, is the entire point. Permit encompass both the *why* and the *why not* in life, according to Linville. "You look at them and realize how difficult they are to catch and ask yourself, 'Why would I try that?'" he says. "But then you look at them and realize how difficult they are to catch and wonder, 'Why not?'"

Many sportsmen and women like to wax poetic about their quarry, an impulse that dates back to the cave paintings rendered by our long-ago ancestors. Not Linville. "Permit are beautiful and everything, but the fact is that success is rare with them, and the less likely the chance for success in an endeavor, the more valuable the endeavor becomes." When one decides to fish with a fly rod, one has already put oneself at a disadvantage. Fishing for permit with a fly rod amplifies the disadvantage, making it perhaps the purest expression of the sport. "They are unfair, but I adore that about them," he says. "Who wants fair?"

Linville grew up in Norwalk, Connecticut. His father founded and ran a sailcloth company. His mother worked as a buyer for a retail skiing company. She is also an ardent angler and was, for many years, the president of the Woman Flyfishers Club, the oldest such club in the country. She was the one who introduced Linville to fly-fishing. Family photos show him holding a fly rod at age five. Fly-fishing luminary Joan Wulff was a family friend. When he was twelve, he got a casting lesson from Lefty Kreh.

Linville's early love for fishing could not keep him out of trouble, though, which began in earnest in his teens. "I had a tremendous amount of anxiety and depression, and the drug abuse was starting and it was horrible," he says. He was kicked out of high school. He tried college but only lasted a few months. "That's when it started to get out of hand," he says.

He moved around, from Costa Rica to Panama to Australia, before ending up in New York City, where he "pretty much concentrated full-time on the destruction of my life via cocaine," he says. Sometimes he combined it with other drugs. One night he went out to dinner with friends, took some Ambien along with cocaine, and nearly had a nervous breakdown, convinced he was at his high school reunion. "I had a complete break with reality that night," he says.

In 2005, when he was twenty-two, Linville moved to Key West, in the hope that another move—and one to a place where he could fish a lot—would help. Instead, he discovered opiates, drugs that torment addicts because of the withdrawal symptoms, the sickness that comes when the high dissipates. "You get addicted to feeling the opposite of sick, that shift," Linville says. Soon enough, he was using opiates and cocaine daily and living a life of desperation. "I lied, cheated, and stole," he says. He sold much of his prized fly-fishing gear to procure more drugs.

Somehow, within that fog, Linville managed to open The Angling Company in 2009. But soon afterward, he says, "it all came crashing down." There were times, he's sure, when he came close to dying from overdosing and suffocating. "With opiates, a lot of it is about luck, like what position you are in when you pass out and if you are able to breathe," he says. He had addict friends die in that manner and in other ways. In 2010, after hitting rock bottom, he decided to get clean and signed over his shop and control of all his assets to his mother.

He quit the drugs cold turkey and entered a rehab program. It took a few weeks to get over the withdrawal symptoms. He worked for his mom in the shop during the days and fished around some docks with a friend in the evenings, at one point going out for a hundred straight nights, "just to occupy my time," he says. It took him six months to feel okay physically, he says, and another year before he felt normal mentally, "when I could rely on my feelings."

After getting clean, Linville set a goal: he wanted to see how good he could become as a fly angler. One way he could do that was by fishing in tournaments and attempting to break world records.

Fly-fishing tournaments and records are anathema to some, violating the supposed relaxing, get-away-from-it-all spirit of the sport. Outside of a somewhat hermetic world, our society has not assigned much value to these two endeavors, not nearly as much as to, say, mountain climbing. In reality, though, if you take fly-fishing seriously, you do it with intent and willingly invite some level of stress, exertion, and excitement. It can mean everything, especially in the moment. And that's the fun. "Nothing you do matters unless you decide it does," O'Hearn says.

The Keys are one of those places where fly-fishing is truly valued. Serious practitioners of the sport congregate there, just as climbers flock to Yosemite and filmmakers to Hollywood. "It's part of the culture," O'Hearn says. "There's one place in the world where there's a framework to find out exactly how good you are, and that's here."

Linville decided to focus on tarpon and permit. The learning curve for the latter was especially steep. "I thought I was a hot-shit fisherman, but there was a two-to-three-year period early on when I was seriously fishing for permit and not catching any," he says. The first one he ever caught in the Keys happened by accident. "I cast my line out just to wind it up, and one ate it when the fly landed," he says.

By 2013, Linville and O'Hearn had started to find some success. The following year, they decided to enter the March Merkin, one of the most prestigious permit tournaments. The competition would serve as a litmus test of their progress—or lack thereof. "It's a lot harder to be optimistic about your own skills when you see, up close, other people who are much better than you are," Linville says.

And yet, in that three-day tournament, Linville and O'Hearn had what appeared to be an insurmountable lead up until the last moment on the last day, when the guide Scott Collins and his angler, Greg Smith, returned to the dock after catching three permit and beat them by an inch. "It was incredibly painful, and the disappointment was all tied up with my recovery," Linville says. "But that was also the point when John and I got really serious about the whole thing."

Getting serious meant getting innovative and scientific about their approach. The first step: a new fly, the Strong Arm Merkin, designed by the fly-tying virtuoso Dave Skok. The fly was lighter than the typical permit fly, going against decades of dogma that insisted that such flies be tied with heavy lead eyes. It allowed Linville to fish with more finesse.

The next step involved creating as much repeatability in gear and methods as they could. In Linville's home in Key West, he has twenty-five rods in various weights that hang from his wall and ceiling. Every rod is the same make and model. Same for the reels and the lines. The idea is to have a consistency of feel. Linville has marked his reels with nail polish at different drag settings so he knows, even amid the mayhem of a fight with a fish, exactly how much pressure he is applying. He has weighed his flies to figure out exactly how they'll sink after they hit the water. O'Hearn also began to track the duo's productivity on the water, the number of permit they caught per day of effort. The ideal number to put them "in the circle, in the hunt for tournaments and records," he says, is one permit per day. (In their best year, Linville and O'Hearn averaged 1.3 fish a day.) They are also obsessive about their knots and adhering to IGFA-legal leaders and tippets. Linville has a tattoo on his lower left leg composed of two parallel black lines exactly twelve inches apart, which happens to be the IGFA maximum length for a shock tippet. (O'Hearn has the same tattoo, but his measures 11 7/8 inches. "Better to err on the side of caution," he says.) Linville also began to wade more for permit, getting out of the boat even in water that came up to his chest, because doing so tends to make permit less wary and can provide him with more—and more effective—shots.

They analyzed every shot taken, whether it succeeded or not. They fished every booked day, rain or shine. (Over the last ten years, they've canceled only one trip.) Maybe most important, they had faith. "If you believe you can do it, you learn. If you don't believe, you don't learn," Linville says. Adds O'Hearn: "The best permit anglers are the ones who believe they will catch the fish they are casting to."

The scientific method and repeatability, in a paradoxical way, are even more important when fishing for an unreliable and unrepeatable fish like

RETRIEVED

175

the permit. "The idea is to push yourself into the things you can control and pull yourself out of the things you can't," Linville says, words that could act as a permit angler's Serenity Prayer.

It's all worked. Since 2015, they have won the March Merkin three times. They broke the two-pound tippet record for permit in 2018. In 2020, while fishing with Steve Huff and his son Chad, Linville also broke the six-pound tippet record for tarpon with a stupendous 140-pound, 4-ounce fish. That record marked the culmination of eight years of effort and is, in terms of tippet-strength-to-size ratio, one of the most impressive catches in history.

One could look at Linville's journey and conclude, understandably, that he has swapped one addiction for another, the classic tale of the recovering addict who, say, runs so obsessively that her knees break down. While there are elements of Linville's fly-fishing that qualify as obsessive, Linville says it's not that simple. "There's a high I get when I fish, of course. The chemical difference between winning a tournament and sniffing a line of coke is probably not that different. But you can't buy that tournament high for a hundred dollars, and the way you recover from it is different, and the withdrawal symptoms don't make you sick. Addiction is not characterized by things that make you feel good. It's characterized by doing those things at the expense of your well-being."

A few years after he got clean, Linville met a woman named Kat Vallilee. (An accomplished angler in her own right, Vallilee holds three women's fly-fishing records, including two for permit.) They've been married for seven years, and they had their first child, Violet, last October. He and Vallilee now own the shop together. "It's rare to be able to have another chance to do things right," Linville says. "I almost died, literally and metaphorically. I have an incredible appreciation for my wife and daughter and the shop because I could so easily have none of those things."

In a way, he says, that appreciation is what drives him to compete in tournaments and chase world records. "I wanted to grab that chance to do something that I otherwise wouldn't have had. It's how I imagine it would be if you were in a wheelchair for two years and someone told you that you could walk again. I bet you'd take up running or dancing."

During our two days together, Linville does not catch a permit, despite some seemingly perfect shots. He's okay with that—for now. It's his first outing since Violet was born. He'll be ramping up his world-record pursuit soon enough.

In the end, Linville says, breaking records and winning tournaments, while giving the journey shape, aren't really the point of it all. "The process is far more important than the result," he says. Process has become an important part of his world: in the throes of his addiction, he was robbed of the pleasure of it. "People underestimate the value of doing all of this with a purpose," he says. "It's hard. You gain a greater understanding of the fish, the environment, the people you do it with, and yourself. There's a lot of joy in trying something for its own sake."

2022

30

The Sportsman

George Herbert Walker Bush enters his sun-drenched Houston suite and breezes past a black-suited Secret Service agent and four employees of his office, whom he greets with a nod and a hearty "fellow Americans." There is a limp in his gait now, the result of a second hip replacement three years ago. But, with an assist from a burled maple cane, the eighty-five-year-old former president keeps up his pace.

Clear-eyed, his thick hair graying slightly on the top and at the temples, Bush pauses at his photo-strewn desk. He's here to talk about football, baseball, soccer, wrestling, tennis, squash, golf, fishing, hunting, jogging, horseshoes, boating, and skydiving. Not watching them, doing them. "Don't forget tiddlywinks and ping-pong," he says. "Those are very important sports to the Bush family."

He lifts his cane. "As you can see, I'm currently on the disabled list." He no longer wades the brawling rivers of maritime Canada, where he once fished for Atlantic salmon. He can't shoot quail or pheasant. He last played a full round of golf in late 2006, before his most recent hip surgery.

But the most sporting man to ever inhabit the Oval Office is only inactive by his own standards. Since 2007 he has reeled in (solo) a 145-pound tarpon, fished with Russian president Vladimir Putin in Maine ("I don't think he could be called an accomplished fisherman," says Bush), played doubles tennis with Anna Kournikova (she hit him in the rear end with her first serve of the match), and hit a two-hundred-yard drive to kick off Tiger Woods's golf tournament. Last summer he jumped out of an airplane from 10,500 feet.

This year Bush is planning to visit the Houston Astros spring training camp, fish the flats of the Florida Keys, and zoom around at speeds of up to seventy miles per hour in the choppy Atlantic Ocean off his summer home at Walker's Point in Kennebunkport, Maine, in search of striped bass. All this will just take him through the month of May. "Sports are good for the soul, good for life," says Bush. He recalls the edgy anticipation he had before a big game in college. "I loved that feeling. I still do."

There's a genetic disposition, it seems. "I was blessed with adult role models," says Bush. His grandfather George Herbert Walker was a scratch golfer, president of the US Golf Association, and founder of the biennial Walker Cup Match. His father, Prescott Bush, a senator from Connecticut, was a USGA president. But it was his mother, Dorothy, a nationally ranked tennis player, who may have been the most competitive of the bunch. "I once complained to her after a poor tennis match that I was off my game," says Bush. "And she said, 'You don't *have* a game. Get out there and practice.'"

Bush was captain of Andover's soccer and baseball teams. He played a year of soccer at Yale, then focused on baseball, where he led the team to two College World Series as a slick-fielding first baseman (Yale lost both). A highlight from those years: in 1948, before a Yale-Princeton game, Babe Ruth presented him with a copy of his autobiography, weeks before the legendary ballplayer died from cancer.

During a career that started in the Texas oilfields and careened through the US Congress, the United Nations, and the CIA to the White House, Bush never slowed down. As the envoy to China from 1974 to 1975, he was known to arrive at diplomatic functions—in a coat and tie—on a bicycle. As vice president to Ronald Reagan from 1981 to

THE SPORTSMAN

1989, he played tennis with Pam Shriver and Chris Evert, golfed with heads of state, jogged daily, and went on quail-hunting trips in Texas.

He even found time for some baseball. In the summer of 1984 former baseball greats Warren Spahn and Whitey Ford talked Bush into playing in an old-timers' game in Denver. When the vice president was introduced, the crowd booed—who wanted a politician to ruin the fun? But Bush started to win them over when he rapped a single into left-center field off Milt Pappas. Bush later took the field at first base. At the plate Hall of Famer Orlando Cepeda hit a bullet down the first base line. "I thought it was going to kill the VP," says Sean Coffey, then the military aide to Bush. But the then-sixty-year-old Bush reflexively dove to his left and knocked the ball down, scooped it up, and threw Cepeda out. The crowd went wild.

On July 13, 1985, President Reagan underwent surgery to remove cancerous polyps in his colon and temporarily transferred power to Bush. What did the most powerful man on the planet do with his eight hours in charge? He played a vigorous match of tennis and, according to Coffey, fell and hit his head and was knocked out cold. "We figured out later that at least for a few seconds, [then Speaker of the House] Tip O'Neill was in charge. But we decided not to tell him," says Coffey.

During Bush's term, the White House became jock central. He played famously fast rounds of golf and bragged that he held the course record at Cape Arundel, his home course in Maine. "People would always say, 'What's the record? 67? 68?'" recalls Ken Raynor, Bush's pro there. "I'd reply, 'No, it's an hour and twenty-four minutes.'"

Bush installed a regulation horseshoe pit at the White House. On one irresistibly sunny day he challenged William "Buddy" Carter, a butler regarded as the best horseshoe pitcher at the White House. "I beat him, 21–0. It was a huge upset. I promised him I wouldn't tell anyone," says Bush. "But as soon as his ass went through the hedges, I got on the phone and called the butlers and said, 'Ask Buddy who won at horseshoes.' To this day I kid him about it."

Sports have allowed this polite man to be a little impolitic. Paul Marchand, a golf pro at Shadow Hawk Golf Club near Houston, recalls a match in which he and Bush played against Arnold Palmer and another golfer. "Palmer was standing over a putt on the eighteenth green, his knees knocked, ready to hit it, when the president suddenly said, 'Arnold, you know if you miss this, we win the match,'" says Marchand. Palmer smiled and sank the putt. Says Chris Evert, "He had this killer instinct on the court and off. He wanted to win at everything, even Scrabble."

Throughout his life Bush has kept competitors in check with a fictitious governing body known as the "Ranking Committee," which adjudicates all sporting events. "It's a secret committee, so I feel a little uncomfortable talking about it," says Bush with a wide grin. He then shows the only known picture of the five committee members, all dressed in different garb—Bush, in a suit, is surrounded by a biker, a woman in a Chinese dress, a man in a baseball cap, and a woman who looks like Margaret Thatcher. Closer inspection reveals that all the faces are, of course, Bush himself. "It's a very effective mechanism for denying young whipper-snappers a chance to get into the big game," he says. He called on the committee last summer when he challenged CBS Sports commentator Jim Nantz to a putting contest. "He got former PGA Tour player Deane Beman as his partner," says Nantz. "They won."

The activities Bush still practices have one thing in common: adrenaline. "I get a physical charge out of [skydiving], and I wanted to prove that old guys can do fun things, too," he says. The one serene exception is angling. "I find quiet and tranquility when I fish," he says. But he still finds a playful side to it as well. "You may be talking to the only guy who ever caught a chipmunk on a fly rod," he says. A Secret Service agent released the rodent unharmed.

Bush has set ambitious goals for the future. He wants to catch a permit—an elusive saltwater prize—on a fly. "Though my wobbly legs will clearly not permit it, I would love to go back to Tierra del Fuego for

THE SPORTSMAN

more sea-run brown trout," he says. He'll settle for a trip to the storied chalk streams of England with his long-time fishing partner, Bob Rich, the owner of Rich Products.

Bush has aged gracefully in the popular imagination. A statesman for most of his adult life, he seemed somehow to embody Jefferson's ideal of the nonprofessional politician. Perhaps it was all a trick of the eye, since Poppy Bush is always on the move. Says he: "Sports have served me well, all my life."

2010

31

The Last American Howler

Steve Huff, his weathered right hand on the motor's tiller, leads us away from the Chokoloskee, Florida, dock in his sixteen-foot Hell's Bay skiff. As the bow comes down on plane, like a man nodding to sleep in a chair, he nonchalantly starts carving turns through what appears to be an inscrutable, watery maze of mangroves.

I'm seated next to Huff, my head down into the chilly wind. In front of us, in his "lucky seat" in the middle of Huff's boat, is the writer Carl Hiaasen. He's wrapped up like an Iditarod musher—ski hat, rain pants, winter jacket, bandanna-like Buff covering his face. At one point, perhaps a bit self-conscious about his getup, Hiaasen turns to me and peels down the Buff. "I'm from South Florida," he yells over the whine of the motor. He quickly pulls the garment back over his face and turns and looks over the bow at the Everglades, the last true wilderness in this part of the world, a geography that is, to borrow Pat Conroy's line, Hiaasen's wound, but also his salve.

There are only a few clouds in the sky, but they are big and cottony and they occasionally blot out the sun. Huff leads us to one of his favorite flats in the backcountry, a spot where acres of gnarled dead mangroves—bleached gray and white by the sun—haunt the horizon, the detritus of 1992's Hurricane Andrew. "Man, it looks postapocalyptic in here, Steve," Hiaasen says. A few blaze-pink roseate spoonbills perched in the dead branches provide a Technicolor contrast to the whole scene.

Fish are around, a few singles here and there. Snook and redfish. Hiaasen, still bundled for now, holds a fly rod in the bow, scanning the water. This is a very familiar scene for Hiaasen and Huff, longtime friends and fishing companions. Huff, the sixty-seven-year-old guiding icon, has a static roster of fifteen clients. Hiaasen is one of them. They fish in concert.

"There's one, Steve," Hiaasen says. He relaxes his body into a quick and perfect cast, two feet in front of the moving fish's nose. He strips the fly.

"Good," says Huff from the back.

"Dammit!" Hiaasen says. The fish, a nice red, has flushed for no discernible reason. "You suck, Carl," he says to himself, then turns to Huff. "I'm sorry, Steve."

"That was a great cast, Carl," says Huff, fishing guide, coach, and shrink.

The fish are particularly spooky this morning, a circumstance that allows Hiaasen to utilize his varied vocabulary. An uncooperative fish is, at different times, a "schmuck," a "butt-licker," a "knucklehead," or a "dickbrain." Hiaasen is an intense angler. He has chipped four teeth while biting tippet. On the bow, even as he talks on a wide range of subjects—shady Miami mayors, stalkers on book tours, the current sad state of bonefishing in the Keys—he is always watching the water, always on point.

That intensity has put him in the top 1 percent of flats fly anglers. A few years ago he caught a 140-pound tarpon with Huff here in the Everglades. In 2004, he landed a fourteen-pound, eight-ounce bonefish in the Keys with guide Tim Klein, just a can of beer away from the fly-fishing world record. On April 1, 1998, while fishing with Huff, he landed a forty-three-pound permit, which would have been the fly record had the tip of his rod not snapped off—which disqualified it—just as the fish was about to be tailed.

He is the author of twenty-three books—novels, young adult titles, and nonfiction screeds—and writes a weekly column for the *Miami Herald*,

THE LAST AMERICAN HOWLER   185

where he started as a reporter at the age of twenty-three. He has sold
more than twelve million books in the United States. All his novels since
1993's *Strip Tease* have been bestsellers. He won the coveted Newbery
Honor for his 2002 children's book, *Hoot*.

Hiaasen's novels are not dense literary tomes. They are fun, fast reads
filled with hilarious one-liners and biting satire (the *Los Angeles Times*
once called him the heir to Mark Twain). But what's most emphatic in the
writings of Hiaasen is the outrage—over our rampant moral and political
corruption and senseless destruction of the environment, mostly in his
beloved home state of Florida, the setting for nearly everything he writes.

This outrage, though veiled in humor and fun, is not heedless. It is
comforting, even emboldening, to read his work and realize we are not
alone, that it is perfectly okay to be mad and exasperated about these
dark forces that seem to have left us defenseless. Hiaasen gives us a voice,
and for this reason he is one of the most important writers of the last
half century. He is our howler, Southern in focus but American—even
global—in reach.

His latest adult novel, *Bad Monkey*, will be released in June. It's set in
the lower Keys and in the Bahamian island of Andros, two places, not
coincidentally, where Hiaasen spends a lot of time fishing (he now lives
in Vero Beach but has a house in the Keys). The bad guy is a Medicare
fraudster, drawn from a depressingly large number of real-life examples.
The hero is the archetypal Hiaasen lead, a flawed but highly decent
character out to right wrongs—a Monroe County detective who has been
demoted to the position of Keys restaurant inspector (known as Roach
Patrol) because "he did something terrible to his girlfriend's abusive
husband with a vacuum cleaner," Hiaasen says. The hero sets out to nab
the fraudster, and we vicariously enjoy the ride.

⚬━━⚬

It's my turn in the bow. Hiaasen remains standing in the middle of
the boat, helpfully providing another set of eyes on the water while
describing an interaction he had with a copy editor at his publishing

house, Alfred A. Knopf. Copy editors, he says, tend to be very literal-minded individuals. This particular one flagged a scene in the *Bad Monkey* manuscript in which it appeared that the hero and a lady friend had achieved simultaneous orgasms. In the margin, the copy editor wrote a note, questioning whether the scene was realistic.

Hiaasen sent the manuscript back with his own note penned underneath: "Yes, miracles do happen."

Fishing was Hiaasen's initial gateway into the natural world. He and his two best friends—Bob Branham and the late Clyde Ingalls—first used dough balls to catch little bluegills, which they called "shellcrackers," in canals near Plantation, where Hiaasen grew up the son of a lawyer and a stay-at-home mom who was a former English teacher (his father died of complications from esophageal cancer at age fifty). Hiaasen and his fishing pals eventually started doing what all those who are hooked do: they sought bigger fish, dragging an old aluminum boat all over the canals of west Broward County to catch baby tarpon.

But just a few years after high school, when Hiaasen was in college (he split his four years between Emory University and the University of Florida), he came home to find the swamps, scrub brush, and dirt roads of his childhood were no longer there. Those canals, once teeming with life, had become fetid, barren drainage ditches. "There were high-rises," he says. "It just happened so damn fast. And once that concrete is poured, it's just gone for good."

Perhaps his most enduring book character was born from that experience. Skink, one of the few Hiaasen creations to appear in more than one of his novels (*Double Whammy, Stormy Weather*, and four others), is an ex-governor of Florida who tried, and failed, to fight the good fight while in office. Frustrated, he walks away one day, unannounced, to live an environmentally righteous, if somewhat unhinged, life as the unofficial protector of the Everglades, subsisting off the land and, of course, roadkill. Hiaasen's friend Ingalls, a misfit and staunch defender of nature who died by suicide at age seventeen, was partly the inspiration for Skink. "The other part of Skink is me," Hiaasen says. "He does things I wish I could do."

THE LAST AMERICAN HOWLER 187

Writing started early, too. He wrote recaps of neighborhood kickball games as a child. In school, he says, he was shy, a recluse. "I skipped a grade, so I was always the smallest kid in my class." He channeled that shyness into a cheeky school newsletter. "All of those big jocks I was scared of, the guys who'd been in school so long they were going bald, liked what I wrote, liked it when I made fun of the teachers and principal," Hiaasen says. "My father always said I was a smart-ass as a kid. It got me into trouble. But I learned there was a certain profitability in it." A first job at *Cocoa Today* (now *Florida Today*) turned into a gig at the *Herald*, which turned into three books cowritten with a colleague and, eventually, his enduring career as a novelist.

But, as I learned over two days on the water with him, Hiaasen does not play into the popular stereotypes we have of writers and their lives. He doesn't really drink, maybe occasionally sipping a beer or two. Rather than going out, he prefers to stay in at night with his wife, Fenia, and his thirteen-year-old son, Quinn. Book tours are done only out of a sense of duty to Knopf. "They drain me," he says. "I do a signing, then stumble into my hotel room and pass out, exhausted." He doesn't drink coffee. And though he is buddies with Jim Harrison and Thomas McGuane, he doesn't even really read all that much. "I wish I did," he says. "I really should. But I'm just so drained by a day of writing." Even when things are flowing, he says, "I'll walk from my office into the kitchen and Fenia will tell me I look like I just came from a funeral."

Writing, despite the toll it exacts, is his high. "I really don't know what I would do without it," he says. It's one reason he stays so prolific, with a book every eighteen months or so, alternating now between books for kids and adults. His expression of moral outrage through his characters—Skink and his passion for protecting the Everglades; Shad, the bouncer in *Strip Tease*, and his pure-hearted devotion to the dancers under his protection; *Nature Girl*'s Honey Santana and her disgust with telemarketers selling cheap land—is, he says, "my therapy."

And fishing, particularly on the beguiling flats, is how he recharges. His best friends are all fishermen, he says, but he often fishes alone. "It's a great reminder of what I do this for."

As dusk begins to settle on our first day, we head back in. Despite the tough weather and snotty fish, we'd managed to catch a decent number of snook and some good-size redfish. We pull into the dock, owned by Ted Juracsik, the maker of perhaps the best saltwater fly reels on earth. Juracsik, a slight and white-haired septuagenarian Hungarian immigrant, is there to greet us. He'd been out all day catching grouper. He says hello to Huff and Hiaasen, and asks how the latter's writing is going. "Good, Ted, good," Hiaasen replies. "Thanks for asking."

Juracsik stops for a beat, rocking back on his feet. His craggy old-world face looks up into Hiaasen's. "You know, I always wondered this," he says. "How in the hell do you come up with the names of them characters in your books?"

Hiaasen just laughs, shyly.

The next morning we head to the mouth of the Lost Man's River, forever memorialized in Peter Matthiessen's Watson trilogy. The plan for the day is to work the flats near the mouth of the river for snook and redfish until the sun warms the water a bit. Then we'll hunt for tarpon.

I ask Hiaasen about his family. His older son, Scott, has followed in his footsteps as an award-winning investigative reporter at the *Herald* (he will graduate from law school this year). Hiaasen married Scott's mother, his high school sweetheart, at age seventeen. They were divorced twenty-six years later. "We just grew into different people," Hiaasen says. After the divorce, he moved to the Keys and met Fenia and married her. Hiaasen became the stepfather of Fenia's son, Ryan, and they had Quinn a year after they were married. Quinn is a crackerjack tennis player who plays "up" an age division in the hypercompetitive Florida youth tennis scene. His serving coach is Roscoe Tanner. Hiaasen expresses some ambivalence about Quinn's tennis, worrying when he sees the young boy tense up because of the game. "I just want him to be happy," he says.

THE LAST AMERICAN HOWLER

At some point in the morning, there is a brief discussion about the burgeoning new world of social media, about its merits and demerits. "I don't know much about it, really," Hiaasen says. "I'm not on Twitter or Facebook."

"I'm so disconnected," says Huff, who does not even have an email address.

"Do you have people who come on the boat and use their smartphones?" Hiaasen asks.

"Not for long," Huff says.

Huff then decides it's time to look for tarpon. Hiaasen is in the bow with the twelve-weight, a big purple fly dangling from his hand. The conditions still aren't quite right: it's a bit chilly, and the sky is crowded with passing clouds, making the black water nearly impenetrable. But we're going to give it a try. A few tarpon have rolled in a likely spot in the distance.

But when we get there, we see nothing. After a half hour, Hiaasen abdicates his spot in the bow and sits to eat his lunch. I stare into the water, fruitlessly. Suddenly, there's a huge swirl on the starboard side of the boat. We've come right up on a laid-up tarpon and spooked it. "How'd you miss that one?" Hiaasen says to me, his smile curling around a mouthful of turkey sandwich.

"Man, we're going to need a horseshoe to fall out of our ass to get one today," Huff says.

The horseshoe stays put.

It's no matter, though. Huff motors us back to the shore to chuck a yellow streamer at the banks, in search of snook. As we make our way there, Hiaasen gazes over the Everglades. "This may be the only spot left here that still looks like it did thousands of years ago," he says. "I mean, it just takes your breath away."

The Everglades and their continued destruction—by Big Sugar, by greedy developers, by compromised conservation organizations—are in some ways the great subjects in Hiaasen's books. The choking of billions of gallons of flowing freshwater to the southern part of the state is "an environmental and economic catastrophe," he says. The deep-seated corruption in the state's government makes it all possible. Hiaasen is no fan of Florida's current governor, Rick Scott, a Republican who spent $74 million getting elected. But he's just the latest joker in a long line. "The Democrats before him were just as corrupt," he says. "I guess it all keeps guys like me in business."

One problem with a denatured state, Hiaasen says, is that it perpetuates itself. "All of these developments are marketed to and attract people who think the high-rises, this concrete *is* Florida. They like the view of Biscayne Bay from their tenth-floor condo. They have no idea what was there before, what was lost."

But he keeps howling because there is hope, which is the main reason Hiaasen likes writing his young adult books so much. "Kids are born with a natural curiosity about nature and real compassion for wildlife," he says. "They like it when I make fun of grown-ups, which is easy for me since it's essentially what I've been doing in my journalism job for years. I won't reach them all, but all it takes is one out of a hundred, one who becomes a purist and goes to the county commission meetings and hollers about some horrible development project."

At the end of our last day on the water, Hiaasen stands up on the bow and repeats a line once uttered by his friend Paul Bruun. "You're only one cast away from greatness."

We don't find greatness, but we do find something approaching it. Snook, mainly in the three-to-seven-pound range, start attacking the fly with regularity. Hiaasen and I get into a comfortable rhythm, taking turns on the bow after every fish caught. The wind has died completely. The moon begins to rise in the east as the sun recedes in the west, spilling bloodred light on the water. There is not another boat in sight, just water and mangroves and sky, a humbling vastness, one worth fighting for.

This is why he howls.

2013

THE LAST AMERICAN HOWLER

189

At some point in the morning, there is a brief discussion about the burgeoning new world of social media, about its merits and demerits. "I don't know much about it, really," Hiaasen says. "I'm not on Twitter or Facebook."

"I'm so disconnected," says Huff, who does not even have an email address.

"Do you have people who come on the boat and use their smartphones?" Hiaasen asks.

"Not for long," Huff says.

Huff then decides it's time to look for tarpon. Hiaasen is in the bow with the twelve-weight, a big purple fly dangling from his hand. The conditions still aren't quite right: it's a bit chilly, and the sky is crowded with passing clouds, making the black water nearly impenetrable. But we're going to give it a try. A few tarpon have rolled in a likely spot in the distance.

But when we get there, we see nothing. After a half hour, Hiaasen abdicates his spot in the bow and sits to eat his lunch. I stare into the water, fruitlessly. Suddenly, there's a huge swirl on the starboard side of the boat. We've come right up on a laid-up tarpon and spooked it. "How'd you miss that one?" Hiaasen says to me, his smile curling around a mouthful of turkey sandwich.

"Man, we're going to need a horseshoe to fall out of our ass to get one today," Huff says.

The horseshoe stays put.

It's no matter, though. Huff motors us back to the shore to chuck a yellow streamer at the banks, in search of snook. As we make our way there, Hiaasen gazes over the Everglades. "This may be the only spot left here that still looks like it did thousands of years ago," he says. "I mean, it just takes your breath away."

The Everglades and their continued destruction—by Big Sugar, by greedy developers, by compromised conservation organizations—are in some ways the great subjects in Hiaasen's books. The choking of billions of gallons of flowing freshwater to the southern part of the state is "an environmental and economic catastrophe," he says. The deep-seated corruption in the state's government makes it all possible. Hiaasen is no fan of Florida's current governor, Rick Scott, a Republican who spent $74 million getting elected. But he's just the latest joker in a long line. "The Democrats before him were just as corrupt," he says. "I guess it all keeps guys like me in business."

One problem with a denatured state, Hiaasen says, is that it perpetuates itself. "All of these developments are marketed to and attract people who think the high-rises, this concrete *is* Florida. They like the view of Biscayne Bay from their tenth-floor condo. They have no idea what was there before, what was lost."

But he keeps howling because there is hope, which is the main reason Hiaasen likes writing his young adult books so much. "Kids are born with a natural curiosity about nature and real compassion for wildlife," he says. "They like it when I make fun of grown-ups, which is easy for me since it's essentially what I've been doing in my journalism job for years. I won't reach them all, but all it takes is one out of a hundred, one who becomes a purist and goes to the county commission meetings and hollers about some horrible development project."

<hr/>

At the end of our last day on the water, Hiaasen stands up on the bow and repeats a line once uttered by his friend Paul Bruun. "You're only one cast away from greatness."

We don't find greatness, but we do find something approaching it. Snook, mainly in the three-to-seven-pound range, start attacking the fly with regularity. Hiaasen and I get into a comfortable rhythm, taking turns on the bow after every fish caught. The wind has died completely. The moon begins to rise in the east as the sun recedes in the west, spilling bloodred light on the water. There is not another boat in sight, just water and mangroves and sky, a humbling vastness, one worth fighting for.

This is why he howls.

2013

Acknowledgments

I f it indeed takes a village, this village idiot has many people to thank . . .

First, to David DiBenedetto, editor-in-chief of *Garden & Gun*, for all his great editing and even greater friendship over the years, and to Tom Bie, editor-in-chief at *The Drake*, who allowed me the place and the space to push myself and grow. David and Tom assigned and edited many of the pieces in this collection, and I am eternally grateful for their faith in me.

I would be remiss to not mention all the editors who have made me a better writer along the way: Sid Evans, Amanda Heckert, CJ Lotz Diego, Dave Mezz, Caroline Clements, Elizabeth Florio, Haskell Harris, Elizabeth Hutchison, Chris Kraft, Tom Post, Alan Farnham, Richard Nalley, Patrick Cooke, Gary Walther, Bruce Upbin, Dennis Kneale, Larry Reibstein, Melanie Wells, Dan Bigman, Michael Solomon, Josh Levine, Randall Lane, William Baldwin, Michael Noer, Mike Ozanian, Lucy Maher Regan, Sue Radlauer, Greg Melville, Dave Scroppo, Tim Bogardus, Sarah Parsons, Dave Herndon, John Atwood, Chris Dorsey, Jofie Ferrari-Adler, Rick Wolff, Gary Brozek, Juliana Haubner, Andrew Miller, Amy Einhorn, Shannon Criss, Martin Silverstone, Kirk Deeter, Colin Kearns, Nick Roberts, Jared Zissu, Steve Duda, Radcliff Menge, Jeff Galbraith, Ross Purnell, Chuck Wechsler, James Babb, Scott Einsmann, Adrian Gray, Ranjay Gulati, Jeff Weakley, Jason Rolfe,

Bill Sisson, Wesley Gibson, Mark Nothaft, Greg Thomas, Paul Guernsey, Adam Duerson, Anthony Licata, Kendall Hamilton, and Jason Stallman.

To all the copy editors (too numerous to list), I extend my deepest appreciation. You are the unsung heroes of this process.

And to all the fishing guides, who are the editors of the angling world.

Jessica Case and Claiborne Hancock (even though he went to Woodberry) and all the good folks at Pegasus are a joy to work with.

Richard Pine remains my lodestar.

The Olympians keep me grounded (most of the time).

My uncle, Charles, is an inspiration and a wonderful companion on the water.

This book is dedicated to my father, DB, who taught me how to fish and whose spirit hovers over everything I do, and to my brothers, Justin and Chris, who rock.

My mother, Hansell, personifies unconditional love.

And, of course, to Heidi and our three daughters, who are simply the loves of my life.

About the Author

Monte Burke is the *New York Times* bestselling author of *Lords of the Fly, Saban, 4th and Goal,* and *Sowbelly,* and the coeditor of *Atlantic Salmon Treasury, 75th Anniversary Edition* and *Leaper.* He has been the recipient of Barnes & Noble's Discover Great New Writers award and an Axiom Award for biography. His books have been named "Best of the Year" by *Sports Illustrated, Outdoor Life, Field & Stream,* and Amazon.com. He is a contributing editor at *Forbes, Garden & Gun,* and *The Drake,* and has also written for the *New York Times, Wall Street Journal, Esquire, Outside,* and *The Daily Beast.* Burke graduated from Middlebury College with a BA in religion. He grew up in New Hampshire, Vermont, North Carolina, Virginia, and Alabama, and now lives in Brooklyn with his family.